ETHNIC CHRONOLOGY SERIES
NUMBER 23

The Filipinos in America

1898-1974

A Chronology & Fact Book

Compiled and edited by

Hyung-chan Kim

and

Cynthia C. Mejia

1976
OCEANA PUBLICATIONS, INC.
DOBBS FERRY, NEW YORK

Library of Congress Cataloging in Publication Data

Kim, Hyung-chan.
    The Filipinos in America, 1898-1974.

    (Ethnic chronology series; no. 23)
    Bibliography: p.
    Includes index.
    SUMMARY: A chronology of Filipinos in the United States
and a selection of documents pertinent to their history.
    1. Filipino Americans. [1. Filipino Americans--
History] I. Mejia, Cynthia C., joint author.
II. Title. III. Series.
E184.F4K55   973'.04'9921   75-43949
ISBN 0-379-00521-2

Manufactured in the United States of America

TABLE OF CONTENTS

EDITORS' FOREWORD

The acquisition of the Philippine Islands by the United States from Spain on December 10, 1898, through the Treaty of Paris ushered in a new era for the inhabitants of the archipelago. By virtue of this treaty, the Filipinos acquired a dubious status of "nationals" under the governing power of the United States. In the true sense of the word, Filipinos, as inhabitants of the islands under American control, were citizens who were entitled to the same privileges and protection as were offered to American citizens, naturalized or native-born. However, in reality, Filipinos were refused the rights, privileges, and protection guaranteed by the Constitution for all American citizens during the period in which they were legally classified as "nationals" of the United States of America, from 1898 to 1934.

It is not clear when the first Filipino came to America proper as an immigrant. But the first sizable group of Filipinos who came to America were college and university students who were known as pensionados, because their education in the United States was "pensioned" or supported by the American government. Approximately 500 pensionados were admitted to the United States for their education, most of whom came during the first two decades after the American acquisition of the archipelago. These students received rather favorable treatment, as they were considered trainees in democracy who would eventually return to their own country.

The present population of Filipino ancestry in the United States, however, results from two separate waves of immigration of people from the Philippine Islands to America proper. The first wave of immigration took place around the mid-1920s, after the enactment of the Exclusion Act of 1924. The 1924 exclusion law dealt a terrible blow to California farmers and cannery operators in the Pacific Northwest and Alaska who had depended upon the Japanese as the major source of cheap labor. Compelled to look for another source of cheap labor, western employers turned to the Philippines and Mexico as a new source. As did their Japanese forerunners, Filipino laborers worked for wages far below the standard pay, and this was reflected in their living conditions. The crushing effects of abject poverty--uncleanliness, unhealthiness, cramped quarters--were attributed to the Filipino race, not to the discriminatory and exploitive practices of their employers.

Racial antipathy toward Filipinos due to labor competition and prejudicial stereotyping increased rapidly and soon the anti-Oriental sentiment in the West Coast was directed toward Filipinos. What made the Filipinos' position different from that of other Oriental groups--especially the Chinese, Japanese, and Koreans--was that a politically legitimate, albeit racist, rationale could be formulated around anti-Oritental activities aimed at pushing for legislation against these groups. The rationale was based on the premise that Chinese, Japanese, and Koreans were aliens, and therefore they were subject to restriction, limitation, or exclusion from the

United States at her discretion, if the circumstances so warranted it. The Filipino, however, could not be placed into the alien category and had to be dealt with in a different way.

There were only two alternatives open to those who sought the final solution to the Filipino immigration problem. One option would be the acceptance of the then existing national status of the Filipino and treatment of him in accordance with his status. The Filipino immigrant would be entitled then to social services and public relief. Furthermore, he would not be subject to the laws that excluded aliens from governmental programs such as unemployment compensation, social security, and old age pension. And these benefits were hard to come by even for American citizens during the Depression. Also, unlike other Orinetals, Filipinos would be free to immigrate to the United States as nationals. The other option would be to shift the legal status of the Filipino from national to alien, thus providing a technically legal basis for his exclusion. The latter measure was adopted with full expediency. From 1924, when the Filipinos began to come to the United States in large numbers, to 1934, when the Congress of the United States passed the Tydings-McDuffie Act, also known as the Philippine Independence Act, the movement to shift the Filipinos' legal status from national to alien gained rapid momentum, aided actively by members of the American Federation of Labor, farm workers, industrialists, and chauvinistic Americans. The Tydings-McDuffie Act, which was passed in the U.S. Congress and signed by President Franklin D. Roosevelt on March 24, 1934, practically put an end to the immigration of all but fifty Filipinos a year. This was because the United States promised, through the Tydings-McDuffie Act, the Commonwealth of the Philippine Islands political independence in ten years, which made the inhabitants of the archipelago aliens.

This sudden and radical shift from national to alien status, however, had its greatest effect not upon immigrating Filipinos but upon those already in residence in the United States. Ironically, the law contained no provisions that should have affected the national status of Filipinos already in America. Those Filipinos already in residence in America entered legally as nationals and their prior status as such should not have been changed by a law the purpose of which was allegedly to control the number of incoming Filipinos. The Filipinos who had entered as nationals prior to March, 1934, were suddenly aliens, and by law devoid of the right to public relief grants as well as the right to vote, to hold any kind of office, and to get white-collar work.

Unable to find a gainful employment to support themselves or their families, denied social services available to American citizens, and saddened deeply by social discrimination of white Americans against them, Filipino residents in America sent to President Roosevelt a petition asking for repatriation. Such a golden opportunity proffered by Filipinos themselves did not go unnoticed by the anti-Filipino exclusionists who pushed for repatriation of Filipinos. Although there were a number of attempts in the House of Representatives to pass a law providing for the repatriation of Filipinos as early as in February, 1933, such attempts did not succeed until July 10, 1935, when President Roosevelt signed into law the Filipino Repatriation Act. From 1935 to December 1940, when the law expired, a total of 2,190 Filipinos were repatriated, at an average cost of $116 per person, from America to the Philippine Islands.

The Filipinos were put into another predicament when the Relief Appropriation Act was passed in 1937. The purpose of the act was to extend relief to aliens who, by some arbitrary standard, needed it. The act, however, was closed to immigrants who did not officially declare their intention to apply for naturalization or citizenship before the act was passed. The plight of the Filipinos in America was greatly deepened. Since they entered legally as nationals, they did not apply for citizenship or naturalization. Now not only was the Filipinos an alien, he could not even take advantage of the patronizing public assistance programs extended to needy aliens.

Yet another disheartening blow was dealt when many Filipinos were expelled from jobs that they had held before the passage of the Merchant Marine Act, which required that no less than 80 percent of the staff and crew of a ship carrying the American flag be citizens of America. Many Filipinos had worked on merchant marine, commercial, and battleships before this act was passed.

All the foregoing events are indelible evidence that the Filipinos became victims of the institutionalized racism strongly supported by legal and political systems in America. In spite of such insurmountable odds against them, Filipinos in America have sustained to date strong family bonds that have resisted successfully the forces working against family unity, have developed a sense of community by establishing social and fraternal organizations, and have promoted the spirit of independence and unity by strong labor movements and collective actions against those who refused to accept them as equals.

The second wave of Filipino immigration has begun to move into the United States as a result of the 1965 Immigration Act, which repealed the national origin quota system that had been the legal basis for immigration policy of the American government since 1924. The Filipinos now constitute the second largest national group immigrating to the United States. During the decade between 1951 and 1960, a total of 19,307 Filipinos immigrated to the United States, and the next decade saw a tremendous increase in the number of Filipino immigrants, who numbered 98,377. During 1973 alone, a total of 30,248 Filipinos came to the United States. It is now estimated that there are approximately 494,169 Filipinos in America, although the actual number of Filipinos reported in the 1970 census was 336,731. Most of these Filipinos live in the urban centers of America. It is reported that approximately 135,248 Filipinos live in ten Standard Metropolitan Statistical Areas in the state of California, as reported in the 1970 census. The Honolulu Standard Metropolitan Statistical Area alone reported 95,680 Filipinos as its residents in 1970.

The Filipino community in America is undergoing a tremendous change as a result of this influx of new immigrants who came to America in search of new opportunities for themselves and their children. Therefore, it is extremely difficult to forecast what kind of basic changes will be brought to the Filipino community in America by changed conditions in its social, demographic, and political forces. However, it is abundantly clear that the new influx of Filipino immigrants will make their influence felt upon their newly adopted country in general, and their own ethnic community in particular in the years to come.

The editors are indebted to many people who have given them unselfish assistance. Our thanks go to Mr. Delfin Cruz, managing editor of The Philippines Mail, who provided us with materials essential to the completion of this book. We are grateful to Professors Ray McInnis and William Scott of the Wilson Library, Western Washington State College, for their assistance in our search for rare documents. Mr. John Eagle Day has given us his precious time. His assistance is deeply appreciated. Generous financial assistance given us by Mrs. Jane Clark, Director, Bureau of Faculty Research, Western Washington State College, is greatly appreciated. Finally, our thanks go to Mrs. Karen Price, who typed the final draft of the manuscript for us.

Hyung-chan Kim
College of Ethnic Studies
Western Washington State College
Bellingham, Washington

Cynthia C. Mejia
Fairhaven College
Western Washington State College
Bellingham, Washington

CHRONOLOGY

1898   December 10. The United States acquired the Philippine Islands through the Treaty of Paris. The inhabitants of the Philippine Islands were denied U.S citizenship, but they owed allegiance to the United States.

1899   February 4. The Filipino-American War started.

        February 6. The United States Sentate ratified the Treaty of Paris that had been signed on December 10, 1898.

        May 12. The so-called Hay Plan was proposed. The proposal was designed to install a Philippine government consisting of a governor-general appointed by the president, a cabinet appointed by the governor-general, and a general advisory council elected by the people. The qualifications of electors were to be carefully considered and determined, and the governor-general was to have absolute veto. The Hay Plan was rejected.

1900   June 3. The members of the Taft Commission, composed of W.H. Taft, Dean C. Worcester, Luke D. Wright, Henry C. Ide, and Bernard Moses, arrived in Manila with President William McKinley's instruction.

1901   June 21. Secretary of War Root issued the order relieving the military governor of his civil executive authority over the pacified provinces and transferring such authority to the president of the Philippine Commission, who carried the title of civil governor, effective July 4, 1901.

        July 4. William Howard Taft became the first civil governor of the Philippines.

1902   July 1. The Philippine Organic Act, also known as the Philippine Bill, passed the Senate. This became the constitutional basis of the Philippine policy of the United States during the Taft era (1901-1913).

1903   August 26. The pensionado program was authorized by Act 854, Philippine Commission.

        November 3. The pensionado program started. In November a group of approximately 100 young, promising Filipinos arrived in California to study in the United States at the government's expense. The name comes from the fact that these students were supported by government scholarship

for their study. Under this program a total of 209 Filipinos
and Filipinas had obtained degrees or advanced training in
the United States by 1912, with a total government expendi-
ture of $479,940.

1905   April. The Filipino Students' Magazine was started with
Mr. Ponciano Reyes as its editor-in-chief and Mr. H.R.
Luzuriaga as assistant editor. The office was located in
Berkeley, California.

1906   March 25. The Rizal Club and Commercial Society was organized with a capital of $15,000. Mr. Eligio B. Villafranca
was president and general manager.

December. A group of fifteen Filipino laborers arrived to
work in Hawaii. They had been recruited by an agent in the
Philippines who was sent there by the Hawaiian Sugar Plan-
ter's Association.

1907   A group of Filipino laborers, consisting of 188 men, 20 women, and 2 children, arrived in Hawaii.

1909   August 5. The Payne-Aldrich Tariff Act went into effect. On
the same day the Philippine Tariff Act also went into effect.
These two acts regulated the trade between the Philippines
and the United States during the remainder of the Taft re-
gime. The Payne-Aldrich Tariff Act was superseded by the
Underwood-Simmons Act of October 3, 1913, which removed
the quota limitations on sugar and tobacco, thereby establishing complete free trade between the Philippines and the
United States.

1911   February 15. The United States Congress passed a law ex-
tending to four years the term of office of the members of
the assembly established under the provision made in the
Philippine Act. The term was originally two years.

1921   January 22. The Caballeros de Dimas-Alang was established
in San Francisco as a fraternal organization.

The Philippine Independent News was published in Salinas,
California. This was the first Filipino newspaper in the
continental United States.

1924   February 2. The Legionarios del Trabajo was organized in
San Francisco.

February 2. Ti Silaw (The Light) was published both in English and Ilocano in Honolulu.

November 1. A number of Filipino students at the University of Washington began to publish the Philippine Seattle Colonist. It was mimeographed in four pages and was published twice a month. The publisher and editor of the newspaper was Mr. Manuel S. Rustia.

1925   May 25. In the case of Toyota against the U.S., the Supreme Court ruled that Filipinos, except those who have served in the Navy for three years, are not qualified for American citizenship.

1927   During the annual convention of the American Federation of Labor, the organization passed the following resolution: "We strongly urge Congress to enact legislation prohibiting Filipino laborers from migrating to the United States, whether by direct route or via the Territory of Hawaii."

March 31. The Filipino Federation of America was formally registered as an organization according to the laws of the State of California.

1928   May 18. Congressman Richard J. Welch and Senator Hiram Johnson, both of California, introduced House Bill 13,900 in Congress for the exclusion of Filipinos. The bill was designed to declare Filipinos aliens.

September 19. A "committee of citizens" confronted two bus loads of Filipino workers at Dryden, Washington, and instructed the drivers to keep going and threatened violence if they should attempt to unload their passengers.

September 21. A group of 200 white workers at Wenatchee, Washington came to a camp occupied by 22 Filipino workers who were warned to leave town. The local police dispersed the mob, but Filipino workers asked the local police for protection.

October 15. Mr. Roman Trias of Seattle, Washington, composed a popular song, "Beautiful Manila." It was sold for thirty-five cents a copy.

October 15. The Filipino Forum, an independent organ of Filipinos in the Pacific Northwest, reported on this date that

a new journal, Commercial Philippines would be published
by the Commercial Philippines Company in New York. It
would act as the spokesman of businessmen in the United
States doing business with the Philippines.

October 15. The Filipino Forum began to publish its first
issue. The purpose of the Forum was announced as follows:
   "a. That this paper is organized in the spirit solely of
   service to the Filipino community in the Pacific Northwest, which is increasing year by year,
   b. That, fundamentally, we have initiated this enterprise not upon pecuniary aim; this is only secondary,
   c. That this paper is intended as the official organ of
   the whole Filipino community, and not of a select group.
   d. That, being unaffiliated to any party or distinct
   group, we shall always remain independent in our policy. Service is our aim, patriotism our urge."

A weekly newspaper, the Filipino Community Press, was
started in Westmont, Illinois. Cessario Tierra was the
editor and Bessie Lois Tierra was business manager.

Fifty-eight students of Filipino ancestry attended the University of Washington this year. Many were from local
high schools.

Seasonal Filipino publications began to appear in Alaska.
One of them was "The New Quadra Gossip," edited by
Antois Velasco, a senior of Whatcom High School, Bellingham,
Washington.

Mr. Silvera Cpistrano, a graduate of Iowa State College,
invented a machine believed to be the first rice planting machine of its kind.

October 28. Seattle Filipinos celebrated Flag Day. It was
the tenth anniversary of the rebirth of the Philippine flag.
Mr. Valeriano Sarusal, president of the L.V.M. Trading
Co., and Mr. Pedro Guiang, a graduate student of the University of Washington, delivered speeches.

October 30. Mr. Juan G. Rodriguez, Filipino secretary of
the Friendly Relations Committee in New York, was invited
to speak before the Filipino Club of the University of Washington. It was reported that he did not receive a very good
impression of Filipino students at the university.

Mr. Juan Urbano, known as the inventor of the Urbano electric pencil and flashlight, left Seattle. He was president of the Filipino Commerce and Labor Council.

It was reported that four Filipinos were attending Bellingham Normal School, Bellingham, Washington.

A house in the university district was purchased for $9,500 for the headquarters of the University of Washington Filipino Club. The purchase was made possible by the aid of Filipino businessmen.

A meeting of all Filipino businessmen was called by Mr. V. Navea, president of the University of Washington Filipino Club, and Mr. Pedro Santos of the Philippine Investment Company to discuss the best means of establishing a clubhouse.

It was reported that twenty Filipinos arrived in Seattle from the Philippines on board the S.S. Empress of Canada.

November 12. A group of Filipinos in Minnesota organized to form the "Filipinosotans" and held a reception in honor of the newly elected officers, including the advisor Professor Quigley, who was a former pupil of the then present vice governor-general of the Philippines. There were thirty members in the association.

November 15. Filipino students in the University of Washington were no longer permitted to use the letter boxes at the university YMCA. In previous years, this privilege was accorded to all foreign students. According to a new regulation at the university YMCA, the Filipinos were also not allowed to use the social room of the YMCA (also previously enjoyed by them).

November 15. Representative Mariano Villanueva of La Union was preparing a bill for the creation and maintenance of a permanent bureau in Washington, D.C., that would handle all pro-independence work and activities.

November 30. According to Mr. Pedro Guiang, there were forty Filipino students in the University of Washington for the autumn quarter. The reasons for the decrease were the rigid scholarship standards and the attempt on the part of the university officials to impose the $50 nonresident fee upon Filipino students.

The first volume of the Bagumbayan, a yearbook of Filipino students in the United States, was sold for $4.00 a copy. It was a recent publication according to the report. The book contained artistic sketches, poems, etc. It was published in New York City.

The Asinganian Club was the name of an association recently organized in Seattle. It was a fraternal association designed to promote the best of cooperation from its members. It was composed of men only from Asingan, Pangasinan.

December 15. The Filipino Forum published the first of a series of articles about Filipino poets in English who were living or had lived in the Pacific Northwest.

It was reported that only nine Filipino students in the U.S.A. were approved as part-time pensionados in the U.S. cabinet meeting.

1929   January 13. A mass meeting of Filipinos was called at the New Manila Hotel by Eugenio Rosas for the purpose of discussing the news stories published in the local papers about Filipinos in the Pacific Northwest. The group expressed the necessity of a closer union among the Filipinos in the Pacific Northwest with a view of effectively counteracting any misrepresentations of the Filipinos or any attempt to insult Filipino pride.

January 21. Commissioner Pedro Guevera and Gen. Frank McIntyre spoke before the Ways and Means Committee of the House and argued against the Timberlake Resolution. Guevera made a vigorous defense of Philippine sugar and impressed upon members of the Committee the sincere stand of the Filipino people against the resolution.

January 27. The Filipino Nurses' Association of Chicago held a benefit dance and made a profit of $118.56. All the funds, except $80 for administrative expenses to push charitable service, was used for helping deserving Filipino patients in Chicago and suburbs.

February 15. Valeriano Laigo was the youngest Filipino businessman in Seattle; he operated the only Filipino-owned grocery store there.

Enlisted men of the Philippine Scouts who had served in the

American army, navy or marine corps for thirty years may
be retired on three-quarter pay under a bill passed by the
American Congress. Sen. Reed of Pennyslvania offered the
measure and further explained that no scout would be paid
until 1930 and the maximum to be expended would be
$250,000.

The Philippine government would henceforth tell students
who were sent to the U.S.A. what courses to study. An over-
supply of physicians and lawyers in the Philippines led to a
shortage of technically trained college graduates...they
would be permitted to study only fish, meat, and vegetable
canning and other such industries.

February 26. Rafino Agoa, one of the recent arrivals from
the Philippines on the President Lincoln, died of spinal meningitis at the Seattle City Hospital. Ten Filipino passengers
were taken ill on their way to Seattle.

February 28. Labor Commissioner Cayetabano Ligot of
Hawaii recommended to the legislature the prevention of
immigration of Filipino laborers to Hawaii, unless they had
guaranteed jobs or unless the laborers had sufficient funds
with which to return home.

Victor E. Nazareth, a student at the University of Washington, wrote a long letter to Arthur Brisbane of the Hearst papers in reply to his (Brisbane's) article charging that Asiatics could not be assimilated into the white race. "You
Brisbane rely on the findings of some of your scientists.
They are white and are often biased in favor of the whites.
(But) . . . for your 'killing power' we have more right than
you have to live in these parts."

February 28. Ninety-eight Filipinos had arrived in Seattle
the previous week and more were expected.

Filipinos in Stockton, California, were trying to raise money
for a community house.

A Filipino student, Dionisio Baldemore, was selected the
best orator at Washington State College. He spoke on Philippine independence.

March 15. A new organization of Filipinos called the Filipino-American Club was created in Seattle Washington.
Vicente Agot was the president.

Lorenzo Zamora was sponsoring the organization of a society in Seattle, Washington that would be called the Filipino Literary Debating Club. One of the proposed aims was to engage in active debates with debating teams from other American colleges.

The movement to find a clubhouse in Seattle for the University Filipino Club resumed. The demands of students from various universities and high schools for a student center was tremendous.

March 11. Three hundred thirty-nine Filipinos arrived in Seattle on the S.S. Madison. They were taken to Diamond Head station in Port Townsend, which was a quarantine station. They were kept there for fourteen days for observation after being exposed to an epidemic of spinal meningitis.

March 13. The Seattle Times printed the following: "Seattle should not be a dumping ground for carriers of an epidemic disease." As reported in the Filipino Forum, the editor was concerned about the men exposed to spinal meningitis and blamed it on the poor examination of the health authorities in the Philippines.

March 30. According to news dispatches from Manila, Senate President Manuel Quezon and Senator Osmena would head a special mission that would come to the United States. They would come to oppose measures designed against Philippine products and to work for independence.

Twenty Filipinos left for Alaska to work under seasonal contract in a cannery at Port Althorp. They were under contract with the Charles Soon Company. (One hundred others were leaving in the early part of April.)

April 15. Two Filipinos died while being detained at the William Head quarantine station in Victoria, B.C. Pneumonia was the cause of their deaths, but both were exposed to spinal meningitis. They arrived by way of a Russian liner, Empress of Russia.

Pedro Guiang was honored by the Filipino community for his completion of a Ph.D. at the University of Washington and for his departure to the Philippines. He was in the political science department.

The University of Washington Filipino Club launched a campaign to acquire $5,000 for the purchase of a clubhouse.

Dr. A.F. Amistad, a Filipino physician in Stockton, California, announced the opening of the Amistad Oriental Hospital, managed and maintained by him. It was the first Filipino hospital in the U.S.A.

April 26. Several Filipino students at the University of Washington organized a Filipino literary society. Its purpose was to promote literary abilities among Filipinos and to help refute false and misleading information against the cause of the Filipinos.

April 30. In Stockton, California, the Filipino Welfare Association, Inc., was making excellent progress in its campaign to build a home for Filipinos. A Mr. N.C. Villanueva was concentrating his efforts towards this project. The building would include a clubhouse, gym, showers, clinic, dormitory, billiard room, etc.

May 6. N.G. Adams of California introduced before the assembly of the state's legislature a resolution to exclude all Filipinos from the United States or at least a sharp restriction of immigration from the Philippines. Due to his status, the Filipino was able to enter the United States freely, but this created competition in the labor market.

May 16. The S.S. Cleveland arrived in Seattle with 320 Filipino passengers. Since February of 1929, the number of Filipino immigrants totalled 2,000.

May 15. Mr. Valeriano Sarusal, former treasurer for the University of Washington Filipino Club Fund, succumbed after a three-day illness. The cause of death was not readily detected. He was one of the pioneers of Seattle and manager of the biggest Filipino corporation in the Pacific Northwest.

May 23. Forty Filipinos died when an overloaded truck they were riding in capsized and overturned on the San Juan Road near Wattonville, California.

May 30. Mr. Timberlake, author of the Timberlake Resolution, said that he was about ready to support the Philippine independence bill.

Five Filipino students graduated from the University of Washington.

June 15. The Native Sons of California were supporting Congressman Richard Welch of San Francisco. He called for the cessation of Filipino immigrants to the United States.

October 24. White workers started a riot in Exeter in the San Joaquin Valley. The riot started after a white man had been stabbed by a Filipino. Prior to the stabbing, white farmers had molested and shoved Filipinos off the town's sidewalks in an effort to intimidate them into leaving the area.

October 25. It was reported that more than 100 Filipinos left for the Philippines on the S.S. President McKinley.

November 4. Seventy Filipinos arrived, among whom was one girl. No death casualties were reported.

November 15. A Mrs. Nator opened another store at the former headquarters of the LVM Trading Co in Seattle. The new store had a dozen billiard tables, barber shop, and a cigar and news stand. Nowhere in town could one buy copies of the Filipino publications in this country except at Mrs. Nator's.

The Philippine-American Reporter was the name of a new Filipino publication in Los Angeles. Amado E. Dino was the editor.

November 30. The yoyo, a Filipino toy, had taken this country by storm.

It was reported that fifty more Filipinos arrived in Seattle.

Representative Knutson (R-Minn.) introduced a bill in the House to grant independence to the Philippines. He described the islands as constituting "the great drawback to agricultural rehabilitation" with which this country contends. Fred Brenckman, the Washington representative to the National Grange, said that free trade with Philippines was injurious to United States farmers.

November 30. Liga Filipina was the name of a new cooperative association of Filipinos, "by Filipinos and for Filipinos." It was sponsored by Mr. V. Agot of Seattle.

Two more publications were announced: The American-Filipino, edited by an American with Filipino associates assisting him and The Philippine Observer, edited by Frank Bolima.

Two Filipinos, Miss Juana Aliac of the University of Chicago and Carlos Quirino of the University of Wisconsin, were contributors to a collection of folk tales of the Orient called, How the Monkey Got His Short Tail and Other Stories.

The latest arrival of Filipinos in Seattle numbered fifty.

December 15. Sebastian Abella, a Filipinos graduate student at the University of Washington, spoke at a recent meeting of the Seattle Labor Council on the problems of Filipinos in the Pacific Northwest. He was the author of a long research study of the Filipino labor problem in the Pacific Northwest, which he pursued under the auspices of the sociology department.

The Filipino Forum reestablished a "Filipiana" section in the paper. It was a section devoted to contributions both in prose and in verse in the major Philippine dialects.

December 29 It was reported that over 100 Filipinos arrived in Seattle.

It was reported by Mr. Will J. French, director of Department of Industrial Relations, State of California, that during the ten calendar years 1920-1929, 31,092 Filipinos were admitted into the United States through the ports of San Francisco and Los Angeles.

1930   The clubhouse of the Filipino Federation of American in Stockton, California, was destroyed by a bomb thrown from a passing automobile.

January 15. The Informer was a new publication that appeared on the Washington State College campus. It was serving as the official organ of the International House. Antonio E. Velasco was the publisher.

Forty-eight Filipinos had arrived in Seattle the previous week on the S.S. President Cleveland.

January 22. Fermin Tobera, twenty-two, was belived to have

been killed in bed during a riot between Filipinos and white men.

January 30. Twenty-five Mexicans were arrested in El Centro, California, for having caused a disturbance of the peace when they tried to encourage their fellow workers to strike in protest against the presence of Filipino workers.

The Filipino labor situation was acute. Wages in Alaskan canneries were the lowest in years. The only hope for relief was a big demand of Filipino labor in the farms of Washington, Idaho, and Minnesota and in the railroads.

February 7. Dr. Hilario C. Moncado, president of the Filipino Federation of America, which had the largest membership of Filipinos of any organization outside the Philippines, was received by President Hoover at the White House. He presented the president with a gold medal in appreciation of his "establishment of international peace and goodwill among all people."

February 26. A ruling by Superior Judge J. K. Smith of Los Angeles, classifying Filipinos as members of Mongolian race (or the yellow race) opened the way for invalidation of more than 100 marriages performed here since 1921. Most of the marriages were between white girls and Filipino men. The ruling did not automatically invalidate marriages already performed as stated by legal authorities, but offered legal grounds for invalidation proceedings to be brought by interested parties in individual cases.

February 28. Over 300 Filipinos arrived in Seattle on board the S. S. President Jefferson.

March 15. Forty Filipinos arrived in Seattle.

March 28. Mariano Marapoa was shot and killed by two Seattle policemen in his room in the Freedom Hotel. According to reports, they claimed that Marapoa attempted to attack them. Mr. Marapoa died with a pair of scissors in his hand. The policemen were exonerated by the authorities.

March 30. A decision was made by Judge J. K. Smith in the Superior Court of Los Angeles County prohibiting the county clerk from issuing a marriage license to Mr. Tony V. Moreno, a Filipino, and Miss Ruby F. Robinson, a white person.

April 11. Before a hearing on the exclusion of immigration from the Philippines before the House Committee on Immigration and Naturalization, Brigadier Gen. F.L. Parker, chief of the Bureau of Insular Affairs, presented an argument against the exclusion of Filipino immigration to the United States.

April 15. The Philippine Literary Association at Washington State College published the first number of its organ, which was called The Philippine Literary Digest.

Another organization was formed by Joe de Guzman in Seattle. It was the Filipino Laborers Association and it devoted itself to the welfare of all Filipinos in this country, irrespective of class or creed.

April 18. Resident Commissioners Guevera and Osias sent a letter to Senator Bingham, in which they voiced protest against the proposed exclusion of Filipinos from the United States.

April 30. Senator Bingham of Connecticut read a letter to Congress from Surgeon General Cummings stating that the prevalence of spinal meningitis on ships from the Orient could not be traced to Filipino origin. The investigation was conducted by the Bureau of Public Health.

May 7. After the mob riot in the White River Valley area (Auburn, Washington) Joe de Guzman, president of the Filipino Laborers Association, conferred with the Japanese Growers' Association and with the police authorities in that area. As a result of the conference, the Japanese growers promised to gradually raise the standard wage of Filipinos working for them.

May 15. Seven Filipinas (Philippine women) arrived in Seattle for the purpose of getting an American education.

June 11. Resolutions calling for the exclusion of Filipinos and other Orientals from Canada and the United States were passed unanimously by the Eagles of British Columbia and Washington at a convention in Victoria, B.C. The resolution was to be forwarded to Prime Minister MacKenzie King and President Hoover. The action was prompted by the unemployment situation.

June 14. The mutilated body of Robert B. Martin, twenty-seven, a Filipino lumberman and war veteran, was found in the woods near Susanville, California. He had been reported "running around with white girls, " officials of the Westport American Legion said.

June 15. One hundred-ninety-five Filipinos arrived in Seattle. Most had signed up for work in the farms and in Alaskan canneries.

June 21. Two hundred Filipinos arrived on this day in Seattle.

June 30. The Filipinos of Detroit, Michigan, had their own publication, entitled the Philippine Independence Journal. It was published quarterly and edited by B.H. Carongey.

July 25. Armed with clubs and other weapons, a mob of whites reappeared in the West Wapato District (Washington) to hang white ranchers unless they discharged Filipino employees.

September 8. A Filipino was nearly beaten to death by eight whites before he was rescued by a white person.

December 2. Senator David A. Reed of Pennsylvania introduced a bill that was designed to exempt Hawaii as part of a general measure of immigration suspension for a period of two years.

December 8. A Filipino rooming house in the Imperial Valley, California, was bombed by a white who was later arrested. Three of the Filipinos were injured in addition to one killed.

1931   Bruno Lasker was commissioned by the Research Committee of the American Council of the Institute of Pacific Relations to make a study of Filipino immigration to Hawaii and the United States.

February 16. The House Committee on Immigration adopted the proposal, on the motion of Congressman Arthur M. Freer of California, to limit Filipino migration to the mainland for two years to 500 immigrants annually.

June 5. Judge Walter Guerin rendered judgment ordering

the county clerk of the Los Angeles County to issue marriage licenses. The decision was based on the ground that Miss Ruth M. Sala was a Mexican Indian and the law of California did not prohibit marriages of Indians to Filipinos. Mr. Gavino C. Visco, the bridegroom of Miss Salas had petitioned after he had been refused a marriage license.

1932   April 23. A group of Filipino strawberry pickers at Banks, Oregon, were threatened to leave by a group of white workers.

May 8. Transient whites seeking employment on the Yakima ranches tried to run out Filipinos in order to make places for themselves.

July 23. About 200 farm workers ordered 58 Filipinos near Canal Point, Florida, to leave town with threats of violence if they refused.

December 20. Congress passed the Hawes-Cutting Act, which excluded all Filipinos as ineligible to citizenship. But it also established a quota system so that 100 Filipinos may enter the United States every year.

1933   January 27. Filipino labor contractors of the Salinas Valley met at Mr. Rufo Canete's camp on the Chualar stretch of highway near Salinas and voted unanimously to incorporate under the name of Filipino Labor Supply Association of Monterey County.

February 19. The Filipino Women's Club of California, with Mrs. C.C. Morales presiding over the meeting, held its regular meeting.

February 27. Filipino labor contractors of the Salinas Valley opposed the attempt of the Salinas Valley Vegetable Growers' Association to reduce the pay of Filipino field workers to fifteen cents per hour during the 1933 season.

February 27. The Filipino Cooperative Association of the Imperial Valley adopted a resolution supporting the Hawes-Cutting Bill. The bill had proposed to give Filipinos their independence at the end of a ten-year period.

March 1. The Rev. Juan Callao of San Francisco relieved Pastor V.C. Guerrer as missionary worker among the Filipinos in Salinas Valley.

March 5. Approximately twenty labor contractors, local businessmen, and members of the Filipino Christian Fellow-chip held a meeting at Borja's labor camp and pledged to donate over $1,500 to be used in building a chapel and community house in Salinas.

March 24. A crew of twenty-five Filipino field workers recruited from Stockton to work on the Castroville ranch, Salinas, refused to work protesting against the change in wage formerly promised by the growers.

April 4. Four men and three women, members of the fraternal order of Caballeros de Dimas-Alang, Inc., in Stockton, were indicted for the murder of Mrs. Marcelina Navarro, who was allegedly buried alive on November 20, 1932, by her fellow lodge members for infidelity to her husband.

April 8. A group of one hundred former residents of the city of Camiling, Province of Tarlac, the Philippine Islands, formed a new organization called the United Sons of Camiling in Salinas Valley. Pablo C. Tangonan was elected president of the organization.

April 30. Filipinos at Chualar formed the Institution of the Sun and Three Stars Aid Association. Mr. A. Concepcion was elected president.

May 15. The Philippines Mail reported that no less than 1,600 Filipinos had left San Francisco port for the Philippine Islands within less than three months. The exodus of Filipinos was triggered by low wages, racial discrimination, decreasing labor demand, and the proposed Dickstein deportation bill.

June 17-18. The Filipino Christian Fellowship held its annual conference and the members of the conference decided to hold its 1934 conference in Salinas, California.

June 26. The California-Manila Import and Export Company opened its offices in San Francisco with a capital of $25,000. The directors were Geronimo Sape, Norris Gaynes, W. W. Leathe, H. F. Hutchinson, C. S. Wagerty, A. F. Cooper, and L. B. Murphy.

June 24. Filipino beet toppers of the Salinas Valley decided to ask growers for an increase of ten cents per ton over the 1932 rate.

July 29. A verdict of not guilty was returned in the trial of seven Filipinos who had been accused of the murder of Mrs. Marcelina Navarro.

August 14. The representatives of 1,200 sugar beet workers refused an offer of the Southern California Beet Sugar Growers to restore the 1932 wage schedule. Although the representatives were agreeable to the wage, they demanded the recognition of the Mexican Agricultural Workers' Union and the Filipino Protective Union by the growers.

August 14. Mr. de la Ysla was elected president of the Philippines Baristers' Association in Los Angeles. One of the first undertakings of his administration would be seeking for Filipino lawyers and law school graduates the right to practice their profession in the state of California.

August 28. The Salinas Valley Growers and Shippers' Association promised that the wage of field workers would be increased commencing September 1. The wage would go up from twenty cents and hour to twenty-five cents. Accordingly, a contemplated strike was called off by the Philippine Labor Chamber of Salinas.

September 25. It was reported that Dr. Fortunato Basalio, a graduate of the University of Washington with a doctorate in veterinary medicine, accepted a position in the Department of Agriculture and Natural Resources in the Philippine Islands and was preparing to leave for the islands.

September 24. A new Filipino church was dedicated in San Jose, California, that was located at 632 North Sixth Street. Rev. Peter Collado was in charge of the dedication ceremony.

September 25. Mr. S.D. Smith organized in San Francisco the Luneta Benevolent Association. Its main objectives were raising the standard of living of its members, promotion of social activities, and encouraging financial thrift.

October 14. Miss Mary Looy was chosen Miss Philippines by the Philippines Mail.

October 29. A conference of California Filipino labor leaders was held in Salinas. They hoped to unite 30,000 Filipino agricultural workers in California.

October 30. Filipino Flag Day was observed in Salinas, California.

November 12. The Filipino community of Dinuba was represented by a beautiful float on the Armistice Day parade under the leadership of Mr. J. L. Santiago.

November 27. Hon. Manuel Quezon, president of the Philippines Senate, arrived in San Francisco with a new Filipino independence mission. In a speech delivered by him in San Francisco, he stated that the idea of maintaining American armed forces on the Philippine Islands is entirely incompatible with true Philippine independence.

November 30. A Filipino organization designed to become at statewide labor body in the State of California was established during a meeting of Filipinos at the Green Gold Valley Camp in Salinas. The purpose of the organization was to promote understanding between Filipino vegetable workers and shippers in Salinas Valley, to cultivate the spirit of brotherhood among Filipino workers, labor contractors and businessmen, and to work for living wages with a view to improving living conditions.

December 10. The new Filipino Labor Union completed its organization at a meeting held in the gymnasium of the Salinas Athletic Club. Mr. Rufo C. Canete, president of the Filipino Labor Supply Association of Monterey County, was elected president of the new organization.

December 25. It was reported that there were sixty Filipino students enrolled at the University of California at Berkeley during the 1933 school year. The university had a total of 11,200 students.

1934

January 13. The Filipino Christian Fellowship held its annual meeting and elected Mr. Francisco Antonio of San Jose president of the organization for 1934.

February 12. Mr. Edilberto P. Jamias was elected president of the Sarrat Brothers of California at a meeting held in Los Angeles.

March 3. A mass funeral was held for the sixteen Filipinos who died from food poisoning caused by toadstools.

March 12. A group of Filipino students at the University of
California launched a campaign known as Mindanao Pioneer
Movement. The movement was to encourage Filipinos in the
United States to return to Mindanao, which was considered
the future granary of the Philippines.

March 16. Labor leaders from Salinas, Monterey, and Santa
Cruz, including Filipino labor leaders, staged a protest
against the antipicketing ordinances passed on March 5 by
the Monterey County Board of Supervisors.

March 19. The Filipino Labor Union, organized on December 10, 1933, demanded from the Salinas Valley Vegetable
Growers and Shippers' Association a wage increase of ten
cents per hour. Field laborers received twenty-five cents
per hour.

March 24. President Franklin D. Roosevelt signed the
Tydings-McDuffie bill, which prohibited the immigration of
Filipinos to the United States. The Philippine Assembly ap-
proved the bill on May 1, 1934.

April 2. Faced with a strong opposition from many labor
leaders, the Monterey County Board of Supervisors repealed
the antipicketing ordinance passed on March 5 by the same
body.

April 2. The Filipino Pioneer Movement was organized by
students of the University of California at Berkeley and the
University of San Francisco at the Filipino clubhouse. The
movement was dedicated to the development of the vast idle
land of the Philippines. Mr. Manuel Cases was chosen chairman of the group.

April 6. A Filipino Circle of America was instituted in San
Jose, California. The aim of the group was to inform members of affairs dealing with cultural, social, political and
economic aspiration. Mr. S. Sabio was elected president
of the group.

April 30. Striking Filipino field workers returned to their
work after a compromise was reached between the members
of the Branch No. 2 of the Filipino Labor Union and their
employers. The wage was settled at thirty cents per hour.
The leader of the strike was Mr. Johnny Estigoy, president
of the San Jose Filipino Labor Union.

May 1. The Philippine legislature accepted the Tydings-Mc-Duffie Independence Act without a dissenting vote. The act was to give independence to the Philippines within ten years after the enactment of the bill.

May 27. A branch of the Filipino Labor Union was officially established at Watsonville, California with Mr. Ray Castro as president.

June 1. A literary and musical program was presented by the Workingmen's Study Club in Salinas. Mr. Sal Sorin, a junior college student, spoke on "Menace to Filipino Nationalism in America."

June 8. Racial violence broke out in the Lompoc Valley between whites and Filipinos. Valentino Reyes, Tranquilino Raqueppo, Jack Reyes and Nemesio Acosta were attacked by whites on their way home after attending a movie.

June 14. A branch of the Filipino Labor Union, Inc., headquartered at Salinas, was organized in Guadalupe with Mr. Nick Losada as its president.

Fifteen Filipinos were arrested as they attempted to pass through Hollister on the night of June 14. They were held for investigation of an assault charge. A Filipino ranch foreman had been beaten allegedly by some of the men held for investigation.

June 16. A branch of the Filipino Labor Union was organized at Lompoc with Mr. Jaime Rodriguez as president.

June 17. The sixth annual convention of the Pacific Coast Area of the Filipino Christian Fellowship was held with nearly 100 delegates from 24 Filipino religious organizations. All sessions of the convention were held at the local Presbyterian church.

August 2. County officers were called to intervene in a threatened riot over the employment of nine Filipinos on the Joseph Valentine ranch. A vigilante committee made up of the Sonoma County Anti-Filipino Association called at the ranch and issued an ultimatum to the rancher, demanding that the Filipinos leave at once.

August 10. A Monterey County Compulsory Arbitration

Board was formed with Dr. E.J. Leach as its chairman.
All disputes arising between employers and employees must
be submitted to the board for adjustment. The formation of
the arbitration board was followed by the repeal of the antipicketing ordinance.

August 11. At a joint meeting of the Lompoc and Guadalupe
Filipino Labor Union branches, held in Guadalupe Park auditorium, resolutions were unanimously adopted petitioning
all employers of Filipino agricultural laborers in the Santa
Maria and Lompoc Valley to increase the present wage rate
of twenty-five cents per hour to thirty-five cents.

August 13. It was reported that Mr. V.G. Torres started
a new business as a proprietor of the Ideal Hotel in Salinas,
California.

August 16. More than 2,000 Filipino agricultural workers
went on strike in the Guadalupe and Santa Maria districts,
the Lompoc Valley, and in the Oreana and Arroyo Grance
areas. The workers demanded a wage increase from twenty-
five cents per hour to thirty-five cents.

August 23. Members of the Filipino Labor Union of Salinas
met at the Oriental Theatre and adopted a preamble and resolution requesting the Central California Vegetable Growers
and Shippers' Association increase the hourly wage from
thirty cents to forty cents for Filipino agricultural workers.

August 27. Nearly 7,000 union men and women employed in
the lettuce packing shed and in the lettuce and beet fields
quit their jobs and walked out in Salinas. The strike completely paralyzed the $50,000 daily lettuce industry. The
general concerted strike was called after the Central California Vegetable Growers and Shippers' Association ignored
the union's request for the appointment of a committee to
confer with similar committees of the union on requests for
a wage increase.

September 1. Mr. Max San Juan, president of the Filipino
Students' Association of the University of California, presided
over a meeting to which Mr. Saturnino Damasco, treasurer
of the association, reported that the club was in serious financial trouble. The club bought a house at $12,000 in 1927
and it had a $2,700 outstanding bill to pay.

September 3. It was reported that approximately 7,500 single men were anxious to return from the Pacific Coast to the Philippine Islands. Mr. Rex Thompson, assistant superintendent of the Los Angeles County Charity Department in charge of the repatriation move, said the number of willing repatriates given above was made in a state-wide survey of forty-two Filipino associations.

September 3. Governor-General Frank Murphy cabled the secretary of war in Washington, D.C., for information concerning the conditions of Filipinos in America. He wanted to know how many Filipinos were employed and idle, their social and financial conditions, and how many of them were willing to return to the Philippines.

September 10. Mr. D.L. Marcuelo, president of the Filipino Labor Union, Inc., stated that 1,800 out of 3,000 Filipino field laborers in Salinas Valley were still on strike demanding a wage increase.

September 11. Approximately 832 Filipino families were on federal relief. Most of them were in California. Brig. Gen. Creed F. Cox, chief of the Bureau of Insular Affairs in Washington, D.C., sent to Governor-General Murphy this particular survey.

September 15. A new Filipino publication, the Capital Filipino Press, a bimonthly, began to appear in Sacramento, California. Mr. F. Dulay was the editor and Mr. V. Quivat, the associate editor.

September 17. Tension between whites and Filipino workers reached a breaking point when twenty white "night riders" warned Filipinos to leave the town of Turlock. Carrying clubs and baseball bats, the white vigilantes visited three headquarters of Filipinos in Turlock and delivered their ultimatum.

September 21. Mr. R.C. Canete's labor camp was set on fire by a group of white vigilantes. The estimated loss was $12,000.

September 24. Mr. Lee Rodrico, a Filipino farm laborer, his wife, and his three children were threatened by a band of white "night riders" to leave the farm of Mr. Joyce, a Turlock resident.

September 24. Mr. D.L. Marcuelo resigned the presidency
of the Filipino Labor Union. He gave extreme failing health
as the reason for his resignation. He was succeeded by Mr.
R.C. Canete.

October 1. It was reported that the American Civil Liber-
ties Union located in San Francisco advertised in a local
newspaper offering a $1,000 reward for informationa lead-
ing to the arrest and conviction on felony charges of vigilantes participating in the raid upon Mr. R.C. Canete at the
Green Gold Valley Camp.

October 1. The office of Camil Osias, resident Philippines
Commissioner, sent an appeal by telegraph to Governor
Merriam of California for adequate protection of Filipinos
whose lives were endangered by vigilantes in Salinas.

A movement to repatriate Filipinos in California was initiated in San Jose by Mr. Max Watson of San Jose, a county
adult probation officer and one of California's leading authorities on the Filipino question.

October 8. It was reported that a petition to be signed by
more than 10,000 Filipinos and to be sent to President Franklin D. Roosevelt was being circulated. The petition had a
special reference to the labor troubles in Salinas that resulted in the wholesale arrest of Filipinos for alleged mass
picketing and in the burning down of Mr. Rufo C. Canete's
labor camp.

The Filipino Protective Association was formed in Fresno,
California. The main objectives of the organization were to
foster better understanding and good will between Filipinos
and other nationalities and to help or protect its members
legally, in case of necessity.

October 15. Mr. R.C. Canete, who had been arrested on a
misdemeanor charge, was released as Justice Harry J. King
dismissed the charge against him.

October 29. Filipinos in Salinas observed Flag Day with a
program of cultural and social activities.

October 30. It was reported that Fresno State Teachers'
College had thirteen Filipino students.

November 5. A general mass meeting of the Filipino agricultural workers was called by Branch No. 4 of the Filipino Labor Union, located in Guadalupe; it passed a resolution protesting against a wage cut from thirty cents per hour to twenty-five cents.

November 15. Branch No. 4 of the Filipino Labor Union, Inc. declared a general walkout of Filipino field workers in Santa Maria and Lompoc Valleys, protesting a wage cut.

November 19. The Department of the Navy admitted a policy of exclusion of Filipinos from the U.S. Navy. There were approximately 1,500 Filipinos enlisted in the Navy, practically all as mess attendants with the fleet. It was explained that the Filipinos were classified as "foreign born" enlisted men. Since "native-born" Americans were jobless, the department decided to avoid criticism by an attempt to relieve employment at home.

November 30. Hon. Manuel Quezon, president of the Philippine Senate, left San Francisco on the liner President Coolidge for the Philippines.

December 3. The Board of Supervisors of Monterey County rejected the $18,000 claim of Mr. Rufo C. Canete, whose labor camp was almost totally destroyed on the night of Friday, September 21, by vigilante incendiary fires.

December 16. The arbitration board headed by Mr. R.L. Adams of the College of Agriculture, University of California, settled the wage dispute between the striking members of the Filipino Labor Union and the Vegetable Growers and Shippers' Association in the Santa Maria and Lompoc Valleys.

December 16. The editors of the Philippines Star-Press, J. F. Galian and Lauro Portilla were attacked by a group of gangsters in Los Angeles during a party held under the auspices of the Philippine Junior House of Representatives of Southern California. Mr. J.F. Galian received a slight stab wound in his right shoulder during the attack.

December 27-31. A state convention of the Filipino religious workers of California was held in Fresno. Approximately 400 delegates attended the convention.

December 28-29. The annual convention of the Mga Amak
Ng Bukid, a fraternal organization, was held in Pismo Beach,
California. New officers of the organization were elected
during the convention and there was a revision and adoption
of a new constitution and by-laws of the fraternal order.

December 29. Miss Frances Gutierrez was chosen queen of
the Salinas Rizal Day commemoration. She was chosen on
the basis of talent, education, and character that represents
typical Filipino womanhood.

December 30. The thirty-eighth anniversary of the death of
Dr. Rizal was observed by a group of Filipinos in Fresno,
California.

1935   January 21. It was reported that Mr. Rufo C. Canete filed
suit against the County of Monterey seeking the recovery
of $15,828 for the partial destruction of his labor camp by
incendiaries on September 21, 1934. The claim had been
previously rejected by the Board of Supervisors.

January 25. Judge Bienvenido Onate Tolentino, a Bible teacher
of the Filipino Christian Endeavor of San Francisco, announced that he was leaving for his education in the East.
He was scheduled to leave the city of San Francisco on
February 12.

January 28. The Filipino Students' Association of the University of California, composed of thirty-four members, held
its open house in Berkeley.

February 13. Governor-General Frank Murphy passed
through San Francisco on his way to Washington, D.C. He
stated during his visit to the city that he believed that an
arrangement could be evolved by which Filipinos returning
to the Philippines might be absorbed in the matter of giving
them employment in many sections of the archipelago.

February 14. A family club was organized in the Sotelo-
Falasco labor camp on Bondesen Ranch, three miles north-
east of Salinas. The club was to meet on Saturday evenings
and a program was to be presented after each meeting. Mr.
P.D. Velasco was elected president.

February 18. It was reported that Mr. Max Watson, county
adult probation officer of Santa Clara County and advisor to

Filipino leaders on the repatriation movement, discussed the California state situation with Governor-General Frank Murphy in San Francisco.

February 18. It was reported that Congressman Samuel Dickstein of New York introduced for the third time a resolution to transport unemployed Filipinos to the Philippine Islands at the government's expense.

February 19. With only one dissenting vote, the constitutional convention approved the final draft of the new Philippine Commonwealth Constitution. Mr. Tomas Cabill refused to sign the constitution.

March 8. Hon. Manuel L. Quezon arrived at Honolulu as president of the Philippine Senate. He was greeted by Honolulu Filipinos on his independence mission to Washington, D.C.

March 20. Hon. Manuel L. Quezon arrived in San Francisco with a draft of the constitution of the Philippine Commonwealth.

March 23. President Roosevelt approved the constitution of the Commonwealth of the Philippines. Attending the ceremony were Governor-General Frank Murphy, Hon. Manuel L. Quezon, president of the Philippine Senate, and Mr. Claro M. Recto, president of the constitutional convention.

April 15. It was reported that Filipinos who left the islands for the United States prior to the adoption of the independence bill but who did not reach California until after the bill was accepted by the Philippine legislature were to be subjected to the restrictive immigration clauses of the bill and were to be returned to the islands. This ruling was made by the Department of Labor.

April 19. The Filipino Catholic Club located at 1421 Sutter St., San Francisco, changed its name to Filipino Center.

April 23. The case involving Mr. Rogue E. de la Ysla in the question of the eligibility of Filipinos for United States citizenship was argued in the U.S. District Court of Appeals. The Los Angeles Superior Court had denied Ysla his application for U.S. citizenship.

April 25. Mr. A.H. Caletisen, president of the Labor Supply Association, presented a petition to the representatives of the Central California Growers and Shippers' Association, asking a wage increase for the men who worked in the lettuce and beet fields.

May 13. It was reported that the Central California Vegetable Growers and Shippers' Association would grant a wage increase from thirty cents per hour to thirty-five cents. The request made by the Labor Supply Association for an increase from thirty cents to forty cents was rejected. The increase was to go into effect on May 15.

June 25. The Senate passed and sent to President Roosevelt for signing a bill permitting the government to provide free transportation for indigent Filipinos who want to return to their native land, but have no financial means of paying their own expense.

June 30. It was reported that there were 54,668 Filipinos in Hawaii, which was about one-seventh of the total population of the Hawaiian Islands. Filipinos were the second largest racial group in the territory of Hawaii.

July 1-9. The Filipino Federation of America held its annual convention at Stockton, California. Five hundred delegates of the convention welcomed Dr. H.C. Moncado as he arrived at Stockton depot from Los Angeles. Dr. Moncado was a keynote speaker for the convention.

July 10. President Franklin D. Roosevelt signed the bill introduced to the House as House Joint Resolution 6464 by Congressman Richard J. Welch of California and approved by the Senate and the House by majority votes. This was known as the Filipino Repatriation Act.

July 28. The Filipino Children's Educational Club was organized in Sacramento, California, by Mr. E. Carinio. The purpose of the club was to arrange musical and vaudeville shows to raise funds for their education in America. Miss Rosaline Galez was elected president of the club.

July 31. Mr. Frank Conner, editor of the Philippines Mail, died of heart trouble in the Jacalitos Sanatorium, King County, California, at the age of seventy-one.

August 9. Mr. D.L. Marcuelo, Filipino publicist in California and editor and publisher of the Three Stars, left for the Philippines on the S.S. President Hoover. His declining health and his desire to be an "observer of political development in the islands" were his reasons for departure.

August 17. The Philippine Commonwealth of San Francisco was organized and the constitution of the organization was adopted by its members. The purposes of the organization were as follows:

"a. To foster and strengthen Filipino unity through the coordination of all Filipino organizations of San Francisco--be it business, religious, social or political;
b. To promote understanding and good-will between Americans and Filipijos through cultivation of an enduring friendship between these two peoples;
c. To cooperate with the arms of law for the execution of justice and the preservation of peace and tranquility in the Filipino communities of San Francisco;
d. To patronize Filipino business in order to encourage Filipino community enterprises."

Mr. D. Guervarra was elected president of the organization.

August 26. It was reported that Filipino residents of Guadalupe were scheduled to begin work on September 2 to build the Filipino Community Center.

September 2. Six prominent Filipinos in Los Angeles formed an organization and called it Secret Six. The purpose of the organization was "to eliminate from society Filipino undesirables and Filipino habitual criminals."

September 6. Melecio Runas and Edmundo Maglaya, both of Caba La Union, were scheduled to leave for the Philippine Islands on the S.S. President Coolidge. Mr. Runas was well known among Chicago Filipino society circles.

September 19. The first Filipino divorce case in Monterey County was recorded in Superior Judge H.G. Jorgensen's Court.

October 9. Beginning with the October 9 issue, the Philippines Mail and Advertiser, two Filipino newspapers in Central California, were issued as the Mail-Advertiser.

October 23. It was reported that the following individuals

had been chosen the ten leading Filipinos in the United States, according to a national survey: Manuel Adeva, Manuel Bofill, Jacinto E. Esmele, Antonio A. Gonzalez, Manuel M. Insigne, Hilario C. Moncado, Louis J. Sarmiento, Vincente Villamin, James G. Wingo, and Diosdada M. Yap.

November 15. Leading members of the Filipino community in Honolulu and Oahu gathered at Moana Hotel, Honolulu, to celebrate the establishment of the Commonwealth of the Philippines, which took effect that day.

November 18. It was reported that Mr. P.P. Umanos, editor of the Philippine Triangle, a weekly newspaper of Stockton, California, was shot to death by Mr. Fermin Goetos. They had a controversy over $240 invested in the publication of the Triangle.

November 29. Mr. Luis Agudo, the founder of the old Philippine Mail, left Salinas for the Philippines on board the Dollar Line Hoover.

December 31. It was reported that there were 5,784 Filipino boys and girls in Hawaii's public and private schools, comprising approximately one out of every seventeen children enrolled.

1936

June 22. It was reported that a total of $2,863.67 was collected as building fund for the construction of the Filipino Community Church and Center in Salinas. It was estimated that the construction would require an additional $3,196.33.

July 9. Frank Murphy, high commissioner of the Philippines, resigned to become a candidate for governor of Michigan in that state's election.

July 20. Mr. Pio DeCano, a prominent Filipino businessman, offered $100 in cash as scholarship to two Filipino students at the University of Washington.

July 27. Resident Commissioner Quintin Paredes stated that he was scheduled to make a fifteen day trip to Western cities to gather first-hand information on conditions among Filipinos in the United States. He said, "I hope to induce those who should return home to take advantage of the Welch-Johnson Repatriation Act giving them free transportation.

August 17. It was reported that there were seventy-eight Filipinos employed by various governmental agencies in Washington, D.C.

September 7. The Mga Anak Ng Bukid, a Filipino fraternal organization,took over the management and operation of the Philippines Mail as Mr. Gonzales left for the Philippines.

Four Filipino veterans received a court decision making them eligible for U.S. citizenship. The Act of Congress of June 24, 1935 (49 Stat 397) provided that "any alien veteran of the World War heretofore ineligible to citizenship because of not being a free white person or of African nationality or of African descent may be naturalized under this Act, if he entered the service of the armed forces of the United States prior to November 11,1918. "

October 7. The Koloa Filipino Young Men's Ang Kasayahan Club,the first Filipino Y.M.C.A. group in Hawaii,was organized. The inauguration of the club was held on December 5,1936.

1937   January 31. A regular meeting of the members of the Filipino Christian Fellowship of Salinas was held at which officers were elected. Mr. H. Della was elected president and by-laws were adopted by the members.

February 11. Hon. Manuel Quezon and his party arrived in Los Angeles. He came to seek an early adjustment of Philippine-U.S. trade as well as to seek a more favorable status of the islands.

March 12. Members of the Filipino Labor Supply Association rejected the proposal to admit non-Filipino labor contractors at a meeting held at the Filipino Community Center located in Salinas, California.

March 13. Dr. Roman Ubaldo,who had received his Ph.D. from Indiana University,became a professor of government and history at Huntington College,Huntington,Indiana. It was said that he was the first Filipino in the United States who became a professor of an institution of good standing.

One hundred and two Filipinos left for the Philippine Islands on the S.S. President Jackson. The number was believed to to be the greatest to go home under the Repatriation Act.

They left a resolution, signed by more than sixty Filipinos, as a memento of their hard experience. The people demanded that they be given American food, proper bedding, towels, and soap.

March 15. Judge H.G. Jorgensen of the County of Monterey sent a letter to the Rev. A.M. Patacsil, pastor of the Filipino Community Church and Center, Salinas. In his letter Jorgensen asked Patacsil about proposed panel members to serve as agents for averting labor disputes by means of discussion.

March 22. The Washington State Legislature passed House Bill 633, which was to deprive noncitizens of the right to lease or own land in the state of Washington.

April 4. The members of the board of directors of the Philippines Mail approved unanimously the establishment of two branch offices; one was established in Denver and the other in Oakland.

April 11. The Filipino Education Club was organized in Oakland by Filipinos with the experience of attending colleges in the United States. The members of the club adopted its constitution unanimously and elected its officers. Mariano A. Favila was elected president.

April 23. Edward W. Cahill, district commissioner of immigration and naturalization, announced that on May 25, 1937, the exemption privileges granted to alien veterans and veterans of allied countries of World War I under the provisions of the Naturalization Act approved on June 24, 1935, would expire.

May 24. Victorio Acosta Velasco, a graduate of the University of Washington with a major in English and former editor of the Red Arrow, an official publication of Bellingham Normal School, decided to return to the Philippines.

May 31. According to the president of the Filipino Community of America, New Orleans, Louisiana, letters were sent to the members of the U.S. Congress requesting them to support the adoption of an amendment to the Merchant Marine Act, 1936, to allow certain Filipino seamen to serve on American vessels. The proposed amendment was introduced in the Senate of the United States by Allen Ellender, senator

from Louisiana, on April 19, 1937. The Merchant Marine
Act of June 29, 1936, included Filipinos in the classification
of aliens who were not allowed to serve in American cargo
or passenger vessels, except within the limit of the twenty-
five percent quota allowed to aliens by the act.

August 30. Mr. David K. Niles, assistant administrator of
the Work Progress Administration, wrote a reply to Mr.
Domingo Battallones of San Francisco, stating that Filipinos
were not entitled to preference to jobs since they were not
U.S. citizens.

According to a report to Governor Poindexter of Hawaii,
the Filipinos ranked fourth in the amount of savings deposi-
ted in Hawaiian banks. Of the 27,576 Chinese in the territory 63.66% had deposits; the haoles (whites) 48.93%; Japanese 46.50%; Hawaiians 29.12%; Portuguese 47.24% and
the Filipinos 37.67%. Among the nationalities, the Japanese
had the most deposits with $12,809,337.85 and the Filipinos
had $4,016,257.03.

September 4-5. The ninth annual convention of the Filipino
Christian Organizations was held in San Francisco.

September 9. More than sixty Filipino members of the Cannery Workers' and Farm Laborers' Union, Local 18257, in
the Yakima Valley, Washington, were chased out of Yakima
Valley by a squad of state highway patrol and a band of organized vigilantes when they went on a strike demanding
an increase in wages.

October 3. A preliminary organizational meeting for es-
tablishing a union for Filipino workers was held in New York
City. Mr. Emilio A. Alba, Jr., a naturalized citizen of
Filipino ancestry, led the organization efforts.

October 3. Victorio Acosta Velasco, editor and publisher
of the Northwest Forum, had some of his poems published
in Christmas Lyrics of 1937, which was edited by Leon V.
Gordon of New York.

October 18. More than 400 Filipinos who came to the United
States in May, 1934, were faced with deportation as a result
of a court ruling against Mr. Esteban Conti.

October 18. Mr. Melecio Toledo, a graduate of the Univer-

sity of Washington with a Ph.D. in political science, was
scheduled to leave for Manila on November 6. He was the
second Filipino to obtain the highest degree offered by any
American institution of higher learning. Pedro Guiang was
the first to complete his Ph.D., at the same university.

November 8. The Filipino Repatriation Act was extended to
December 31, 1938. It was reported that 750 Filipinos had
returned to the islands.

November 22. A total of 165 Filipinos were repatriated to
the Philippines on the S.S. President Hoover from San Francisco. Among them were 102 Filipinos who were repatriated
at U.S. government expense.

December 13. The Filipino League for Social Justice was
organized in Washington, D.C. The league was headed by
Dr. B.M. Gancy.

1938   January 7. The Filipino Labor Supply Association of Monterey County held it election and elected Filipe B. San as
its president.

January 17. In a letter to Senator Copeland, Resident Commissioner Quintin Paredes argued that the Filipinos were
not aliens.

January 18. In response to derogatory remarks made by
Congressman Richard J. Welch of California, in a previous
hearing before the Committee on Merchant Marine for the
House of Representatives, Dr. B.M. Gancy, director of the
League of Social Justice, defended the Filipinos' stance.

January 24. It was reported that 600 Filipinos were hired
back into pullman car service as a result of concerted action by friends of Filipinos in Denver, Colorado.

January 24. The Filipino farmers of the Imperial Valley
had 450 acres planted in tomatoes, squash, cantaloupes, and
cucumbers as of 1938.

February 1. Mr. Maximo Escalante died of pneumonia at
the St. Claire's Hospital in New York He had served as a
correspondent for the Philippines Mail.

February 14. Mr. Moises Abaquita was put on the honor

list at the University of Washington. He came from Talisay, Cebu, to the United States in 1929.

February 25. Resident Commissioner Quintin Paredes repudiated the League for Social Justice. Paredes stated in his released statement that he could not endorse the league.

March 7. Mr. Pedro T. Orata, Ph.D., former superintendent of schools of Isabella and Sorsogon, Philippine Islands, was selected for inclusion in Who's Who in American Education.

March 14. The Filipino community of Sacramento planned to have a community center. Mr. Elias Cabradilla led the movement.

March 24-26. The First Filipino National Conference in the United States was held with about 2,000 delegates in attendance at Sacramento, California.

April 4. Florentino S. Lamug was employed to sing for the KFQD, a radio station in Alaska, after his graduation from the University of Washington.

June 4. A benefit dance was held in New York under the auspices of the Visayan Circle of New York. The organization had 200 active members.

June 20. Albert L. Reyes, president of the Filipino Labor Union of Guadalupe, who had been apprehended in Honolulu on his way to the Philippine Islands, was to be returned to the mainland to face charges of embezzlement involving more than $1,500, according to Attorney Weldon of Santa Maria County.

July 4. During a raid of San Francisco Chinatown gambling houses that was led by District Attorney Anthony Brazil, more than 200 Filipinos were rounded up and 7 Chinese were arrested.

July 8. Julius B. Ruiz, a correspondent for the Philippines Mail, filed a report from Alaska that stated that approximately 1,500 Filipinos were to work in the salmon canneries in Alaska during the summer of 1938.

August 8. The California State Supreme Court upheld a de-

cision by the Superior Court of Monterey County that had
ruled that Luis Agudo, claimant, was not entitled to $7,765
for damages he had suffered from the burning of the bunk-
house of Mr. Rufo C. Canete.

November 4. Members of the Filipino Federation of America
held a banquet in honor of their leader, Hilario C. Moncado,
on his fortieth birthday.

1939

January 3. Mr. Joaquin M. Elizalde was sworn in at the
opening of the seventy-sixth Congress as resident commissioner of the Philippines to the United States by Speaker
William B. Bankhead.

January 22. Mr. Francisco Varona, a labor leader and newspaper editor in the Philippines, arrived in the United States
to work as assistant to Resident Commissioner Elizalde at
Washington, D.C. He was expected to work toward improving the Filipino situation in the United States.

January 23. The Filipino Benevolent Club was organized by
G.S. Gerona of Salinas. The aims of the organization were
to help deserving members in distress, to encourage the
members to patronize Filipino business, to cooperate with
city, county, and state officials, and to fight for the legal
rights of deserving members.

January 23. Mr. Trinidad A. Rojo, a doctoral student at the
University of Washington, proposed to Mr. Varona the establishment of a community council in every Filipino community.

March 13. Under the leadership of Mr. J. Posadas Estacio,
the Filipino Farmers' Association of Central California was
organized in Pismo Beach. S. Valdez was elected president.

March 22. Francisco Varona flew to California to conduct
negotiations between the asparagus workers on strike and
the growers of Stockton and Sacramento. The workers were
granted their demand for at least $1.10 per hundred pounds
of asparagus.

April 2. The Filipino asparagus workers of the Stockton
and Sacramento valleys formed the Filipino Agricultural
Workers Association to defend their rights, according to
Macario Bautista, president of the organization.

May 27. Mr. Trinidad Rojo became a candidate for the
presidency of the United Cannery, Agricultural Packing and
Allied Workers of America, Local 7, CIO of Seattle Washington.

May 27. The Filipino CIO leaders of Seattle, Washington,
won a payroll increase over the 1938 wage scale, amounting
to $500,000 for 1939. The increase ranged from $27.50 to
$100 a month.

June 30. The Filipino Journal was published by the Filipino
Agricultural Workers Union, which was led by Dr. Macario
Bautista. The journal was published in Stockton by J.C. Dionesio, who once served as editor of the defunct Filipino Pioneer.

July 1-8. The Filipino Federation of America held its fourteenth annual meeting in Stockton, California.

July 27. A second repatriation act was signed into law. This
was to be executed by the attorney general, the secretary
of the navy and officers of the Immigration and Naturalization Service.

August 5. Several members of the Filipino community of
San Francisco declared illegal the election held on August
5, and they published their letter of protest in the Philippines Mail on August 30, 1939.

August 28. An agreement between Japanese farmer and Filipino farm workers in the counties of Yolo, Sonoma, Placer,
Contra Costa, Yuba, and Sacramento was reached to set the
hourly wage of Filipino workers at thirty-five cents.

September 29. Dr. Macario D. Bautista, president of the
Filipino Agricultrual Laborers' Association of Stockton, was
robbed of $10,000 at gunpoint by three Filipinos.

October 16. Mr. Trinidad Rojo was elected president of the
CIO Local 7 in the election held in Seattle, Washington.

November 11-12. The ninth annual convention of the Filipino
Christian Organizations was held in Salinas, California.
Manuel M. Insigne, executive editor of the Philippines Mail,
was the keynote speaker.

May 27. Mr. Trinidad Rojo became a candidate for the presidency of the United Cannery, Agricultural Packing and Allied Workers of America, Local 7, CIO of Seattle Washington.

May 27. The Filipino CIO leaders of Seattle, Washington, won a payroll increase over the 1938 wage scale, amounting to $500,000 for 1939. The increase ranged from $27.50 to $100 a month.

June 30. The Filipino Journal was published by the Filipino Agricultural Workers Union, which was led by Dr. Macario Bautista. The journal was published in Stockton by J.C. Dionesio, who once served as editor of the defunct Filipino Pioneer.

July 1-8. The Filipino Federation of America held its fourteenth annual meeting in Stockton, California.

July 27. A second repatriation act was signed into law. This was to be executed by the attorney general, the secretary of the navy and officers of the Immigration and Naturalization Service.

August 5. Several members of the Filipino community of San Francisco declared illegal the election held on August 5, and they published their letter of protest in the Philippines Mail on August 30, 1939.

August 28. An agreement between Japanese farmer and Filipino farm workers in the counties of Yolo, Sonoma, Placer, Contra Costa, Yuba, and Sacramento was reached to set the hourly wage of Filipino workers at thirty-five cents.

September 29. Dr. Macario D. Bautista, president of the Filipino Agricultrual Laborers' Association of Stockton, was robbed of $10,000 at gunpoint by three Filipinos.

October 16. Mr. Trinidad Rojo was elected president of the CIO Local 7 in the election held in Seattle, Washington.

November 11-12. The ninth annual convention of the Filipino Christian Organizations was held in Salinas, California. Manuel M. Insigne, executive editor of the Philippines Mail, was the keynote speaker.

cision by the Superior Court of Monterey County that had
ruled that Luis Agudo, claimant, was not entitled to $7,765
for damages he had suffered from the burning of the bunk-
house of Mr. Rufo C. Canete.

November 4. Members of the Filipino Federation of America
held a banquet in honor of their leader, Hilario C. Moncado,
on his fortieth birthday.

1939   January 3. Mr. Joaquin M. Elizalde was sworn in at the
opening of the seventy-sixth Congress as resident commissioner of the Philippines to the United States by Speaker
William B. Bankhead.

January 22. Mr. Francisco Varona, a labor leader and newspaper editor in the Philippines, arrived in the United States
to work as assistant to Resident Commissioner Elizalde at
Washington, D.C. He was expected to work toward improving the Filipino situation in the United States.

January 23. The Filipino Benevolent Club was organized by
G.S. Gerona of Salinas. The aims of the organization were
to help deserving members in distress, to encourage the
members to patronize Filipino business, to cooperate with
city, county, and state officials, and to fight for the legal
rights of deserving members.

January 23. Mr. Trinidad A. Rojo, a doctoral student at the
University of Washington, proposed to Mr. Varona the establishment of a community council in every Filipino community.

March 13. Under the leadership of Mr. J. Posadas Estacio,
the Filipino Farmers' Association of Central California was
organized in Pismo Beach. S. Valdez was elected president.

March 22. Francisco Varona flew to California to conduct
negotiations between the asparagus workers on strike and
the growers of Stockton and Sacramento. The workers were
granted their demand for at least $1.10 per hundred pounds
of asparagus.

April 2. The Filipino asparagus workers of the Stockton
and Sacramento valleys formed the Filipino Agricultural
Workers Association to defend their rights, according to
Macario Bautista, president of the organization.

June 6. Testifying before the House Committee on Merchant
Marine and Fisheries, Resident Commissioner J.M. Elizalde
made an appeal on behalf of Filipino seamen who would be
deprived of their livelihood by the passage of House Resolution 9918 which provided that pilots, officers, and crew of
vessels documented under the laws of the United States shall
be citizens of the United States, either native-born or naturalized.

July 20-21. Francisco Varona, chief of the Nationals Division
of the Philippine Resident Commissioner's Office, called a
conference of Filipino communities in California. The Filipino community of San Francisco played host to the two-day
conference.

August 22-25. Filipino communities across the United States
sent to Washington, D.C. their athletic delegations to participate in the first Filipino national athletic competition.
California delegates won four events.

August 27. In spite of the opposition put up by Philippine
Resident Commissioner J.M. Elizalde, all Filipinos in the
United States were required to register and be finger-prin-
ted as "aliens, " between August 27 and December 26, 1940.

October 1. All Filipino civil service employees who had
been in the service of the federal government for at least
three years were offered the right to become United States
citizens, according to a last minute amendment to the Nationality Act of 1940, offered by Senator William H. King of
Utah.

November 23. The second annual Filipino Inter-Community
Conference was held in Salinas. Delegates from fifteen Filipino community organizations in California met at the conference.

The efforts to repatriate Filipinos ceased with the passage
of the Nationality Act of 1940.

1941   January 5. The Filipinos in Sacramento, California, held an
election and elected Mr. Victor E. Bacho as their president.
One of his goals during his tenure was the goal of building
a community center for Filipinos in that city.

January 21.   Francisco Varona was criticized by members

November 13. Filipino leaders of Sacramento gathered to-gether to form a branch of the Committee for the Protection of Filipino Rights in the United States. The aim of the com-mittee, among others, was to help pass a bill pending in a committee of the U.S. Congress. The bill, known as H.R. 7239, was introduced by Representative Vito Marcantonio of New York. The bill was to enable Filipinos who came to the United States prior to April 1934, and who would reside per-manently, to become naturalized citizens.

1940   January 19-22. The ninth national convention of the Cabal-leros de Dimas Alang of American was held in Sacramento.

February 12. The salmon cannery industry, which had a gross annual income of $50,000,000, conceded exclusive bar-gaining agency to the Cannery Workers and Farm Laborers' Union, the Seattle Local of the United Cannery, Agricultural Packing and Allied Workers of America, a branch of the CIO.

March 3. Filipinos in Salinas, California, held an election to elect their community leader. Mr. Macario G. Collado was elected president and Mr. Florencio Galope was elected vice-president.

April 30. Mr. Pio DeCano, a Seattle cannery contractor, won a court case pertaining to the right of Filipinos to own real estate in the state of Washington. Superior Judge Donald McDonald of Seattle stated in his memorandum decision: "Clearly Filipinos were not within the purview of the anti-alien Act of 1921, because they were not aliens. Matters of citizenship, naturalization, immigration and alienage are ex-clusively under the jurisdiction of the Federal government. All of the decisions of the Federal Courts hold that they (Filipinos) are not aliens, but are American nationals."

May 28. Mr. John J. McGrath, district commissioner of im-migration and naturalization, San Francisco district, came to Salinas and held a public meeting where he explained the repatriation act.

June 5. In connection with the executive order of the presi-dent of the United States, the Immigration and Naturalization Service advised that Filipinos who came to the United States after May 1, 1934, and had established permanent residence should secure a reentry permit from the Immigration and Naturalization Service before leaving the country.

of the Filipino Agricultural Labor Association for his leadership in affiliating the FALA with the American Federation of Labor.

March 2. Mrs. Eugenia Sales was elected president of the Filipino community of Salinas Valley.

April 2. The members of the Federated Agricultural Laborers' Association, Local No. 22494, an affiliate of the A.F.L., were on strike against the asparagus growers in Stewart Tract, Union Island, Roberts Island, and Victoria Island.

May 12. The Vegetable Growers and Shippers' Association of Central California, which employed more than 6,000 Filipino field workers, approved the request by the Filipino Labor Supply Association for a five cents per hour wage increase.

June 25. More than 10,000 Filipinos, dressed in their native costumes, marched through Pronepal Street of Hilo, Hawaii, carrying lanterns and banners bearing the inscription, "We are loyal to America."

June 27-29. The third Filipino Inter-community Conference was held in Oakland, California, and Francisco Varona was to be invited to deliver a keynote speech.

June 28. Francisco Varona, chief of the Nationals Division of the Philippine Resident Commissioner's Office, died of cerebral hemorrhage at the Polyclinic Hospital in New York.

August 18. Mr. Manuel A. Adeva was appointed to succeed the late Mr. Francisco Varona.

August 23. Memorial services were performed over the remains of the late Mr. Varona on board the S.S. Dona Ancita, one of the Madrigal ships of the Philippines.

September 6. Governor Culbert L. Olson of California, honored Philippine Day at the Sacramento State Fair.

November 30. President Manuel Quezon declared that the outbreak of war in the Pacific would find Filipinos unprepared and the civilian population unprotected.

December 7. Japan made a surprise attack on Pearl Harbor.

December 9. The Senate of the United States passed an act to authorize the employment of nationals of the United States on any public work of the United States in the Territory of Hawaii.

December 14. Portland Filipinos held a mass meeting and deliberated how best they could assist the cause of their country.

December 20. The Congress of the United States passed Public Law 360 enabling Filipinos to serve in the army of the United States.

1942 January 5. Mr. Juan B. Sarmiento, chairman of the Committee on Resolution on the Formation of the Filipino Army, sent a letter to the secretary of war informing him of the formation of the Filipino army units.

January 28. A total boycott against the Japanese was agreed upon to carry out the first mandate of the Filipino Committee of Salinas Valley, which was established at the outbreak of the Pacific war.

March 28. Gabriel Q. Arellano, president and founder of the Filipino National Alliance, made an important announcement to all Filipino organizations in the United States that his alliance had respectively petitioned the Congress of the United States to approve the Filipino naturalization bill introduced by Representative Vito Marcantonio of New York. The bill was known as H.R. 1844.

April 22. The War Department activated the formation of the First Filipino Infantry Battalion, U.S. Army, by the arrival in Camp San Luis Obispo of three officers of the Philippine Army. The outfit was under the command of Lieut. Col. Robert H. Offley, U.S. Infantry, who was an officer of the U.S. Army.

May 14. The deferment of military service for the Filipino cannery workers was considered by the national headquarters of the Selective Service System.

May 15. The Gallup Poll was to determine whether or not the Filipino naturalization bill, officially known as H.R. 1844, had popular support from American voters.

June 25-28. No less than forty-two Filipino communities in the United States were represented at the fourth Filipino Inter-Community Conference in Los Angeles.

August 2. The Third Battalion, Filipino Unit, of the California State Militia of Salinas, received its colors.

December 24. The Filipino Forum was reissued. The national crisis and the demand for well-guided public opinion were the incentives to continue the paper.

1943   January 15. President Roosevelt's order deferring those who were over thirty years old made the prospect for that year's operation of Alaska salmon canneries brighter than ever before. According to statistical tabulation prepared by Mr. Trinidad Rojo, based on the data found in the applications of 1942, 55 percent of former workers were thirty years old.

January 31. The Filipinos in Sacramento held an election and elected Isidro Navarro as their president for the 1943-44 period.

February 15. Filipino farmers in the White River Valley organized the Valley Vegetable Growers Association, which had the following aims: (1) to have a better understanding among farmers to solve collectively their individual problems, (2) to cooperate more effectively with the government in the production of food for the war effort, and (3) to make farming a profitable business by pooling their purchases of all their agricultural needs and by centralized marketing of their crops.

February 15. It was reported that Carlos Romulo visited Seattle during the month of February.

March 5. The Filipino Center, established as a meeting and recreational place for Filipinos in the metropolitan area of New York, was opened.

April 9. The nationals of the United States and citizens of the Philippines were no longer barred by the California Alien Property Initiative Act of 1920 from holding real property in California, according to an opinion rendered by Robert W. Kenny, attorney-general of California.

July 1-4. The fifth annual Filipino Inter-Community Conference was held in Stockton, California.

September 27. Seattle Filipinos subscribed to a total of
$107,925 worth of war bonds.

December 9. The Senate passed Senate Joint Resolution 93
granting Philippine independence by presidential proclama-
tion immediately after the Japanese had been driven out of
the islands and normal conditions restored.

1944   April 29. Col. Carlos P. Romulo, secretary of information
and public relations of the Commonwealth of the Philippines,
went to address thirteen Filipino communities in California
and Arizona as personal envoy of President Quezon.

May 18. A bill to authorize the naturalization of Filipinos
was introduced in the House of Representatives by Dan R.
McGehee of Meadville, Mississippi.

June 7. Mr. Vincent Lim, Jr., son of the former Brig.Gen.
Lim of the Philippine Army of Bataan fame, graduated from
West Point.

June 27. Col. Carlos P. Romulo secured a pledge in favor
of Philippine freedom from the Republican party through its
spokesman. Governor Earl Warren, temporary chairman of
the Republican party convention, made the pledge.

July 1-9. The Filipino Federation of America held its nineteenth annual convention in Stockton under the leadership of
acting president, Mr. E.C. Pecson.

July 14. President Quezon appointed seven prominent Filipinos to the Philippine Rehabilitation Commission.

August 1. Hon. Manuel Luiz Quezon died at the age of sixty-
six.

Mr. Sergio Osmena took the oath of office in Washington,
D.C., as president of the Philippines.

August 29. Col. Carlos P. Romulo, new resident commissioner of the Philippines to the United States, delivered his
first address on the floor of Congress of the United States
on the twenth-eighth anniversary of the passage of the Jones
Act.

September 11-14. The sixth Filipino Inter-Community Conference was held in Fresno, California.

1945   January 1. The California State Legislature was in session and the Filipinos who said that they were interested in securing legislation to eliminate discrimination against them and to define their rights more clearly were working to secure the legislation.

Many Filipinos believed the last Congress had passed the bill authorizing the right for them to become citizens. They were mistaken -- it died in the seventy-eighth Congress. Congressman LeRoy Johnson (Stockton, California) opposed its consideration.

Manuel M. Insigne, formerly the executive editor of the Mail, accepted the appointment as coordinator of labor relations inthe Philippine government in exile. He was also designated as a member of the President's Technical Committee to work with the Filipino Rehabilitation Commission. He was to work with anything connected with the welfare of Filipino labor.

The Philippine Cultural Society was launched by Francisco A. Lopez with a big and successful program in Los Angeles.

Under the existing orders, thousands of Filipinos were subject to the draft. This included farmers and farm hands. The army needed more men to make up for the casualties. However, Mr. Herbert Spoor of the Department of Agriculture War Board, Berkeley, expressed the opinion that, under the Tydings amendment to the Selective Service Act, farmers and farm hands active in their work might still be deferred.

March. Bitter Tears of Mother Philippines, a book that was to become a bestseller, was placed in bookstores. It was written by Evaristo Pecson, who also wrote Our World. Mr. Pecson was nominated by the Mail for a diplomatic position to represent the Philippines at a world peace conference after the war.

President S. Osmena was expected to ask the service of Filipinos who could render services to the Philippine government in the United States and the Philippines. Captain A. Cruz was considered and sent to Hawaii to survey the needs and conditions of Filipinos there. Mr. Evaristo Pec-

son was working in connection with diplomacy and postwar
peace.

Mr. Antonio Cruz, labor leader in Stockton, California, was
appointed by Mr. Francis H. Wood, area representative of
the California WFA wage board, as his assistant.

1945

Representative John Rankin of Mississippi objected to the
Citizenship Bill (McGehee Bill, HR 776), so its consideration was delayed to April 2. The Filipino International Community, headed by A.A. Gonzales, was interested in passing
the bill.

From New York City, the News owned by Mr. J. Patterson
and the Washington Times-Herald, proposed that the Philippines should be made the forty-ninth state. In their editor-
ials, they credit Filipino loyalty and cooperation. Also the
Philippines could be an outpost for the United States in the
Pacific. The proposal caused a minor sensation.

May. The Filipino mayor of Oakland, Mr. Joe Budhi, was a
successful businessman in the Bay Area and one of the rich-
est Filipinos in California. He was the general chairman of
the Silver Jubilee of the Caballeros dimas Alang.

May 22. The Supreme Court ruled that the Filipinos were
not alien. Filipinos were now permitted to own real estate
because they were United States nationals and did not come
under the State Alien Land Act.

June. On behalf of the Caballeros dimas Alang, Mr. C.T.
Alfafara, grand master, presented Carlos Romulo with a
check for $4,568.50 for the relief of the Philippines.

August. It was reported by the Mail that the Philippine-American Chamber of Commerce of New York City did not have
a single Filipino member. In fact, it discouraged dealings
or contacts with Filipinos. It was composed of Americans,
Englishmen, and Spaniards.

October. Mr. Trinidad Rojo, substituting for Dr. M. Kalaw,
lectured on the Philippine people and culture at Columbia
University. He had previously lecutred at the University of
Washington for the sociology department.

November. The Laughter of My Father, by Carlos Bulosan,

published in 1944 by Harcourt, Brace and Company, was to
come out in pocket size form under Grosset and Dunlap.

1946   January. It was announced in the Mail, that a Roxas for
President Club in America was formed. It was headed by
A. Escalona of Delano, California.

March. President Truman approved HR 5138, which would
transfer $200,000,000 for the pay of the army of the Fili-
pinos. The effect was to bar Philippine Army veterans from
all benefits under the G.I. Bill of Rights with the exception
of disability and death benefits, which were paid on the basis
of one peso per dollar of eligible benefits.

April. Virginia Velez of St. Mary's High School, Stockton,
California, entered the Pepsi-Cola Scholarship contest then
being run nationwide. She was chosen because of her outstanding academic achievements. Virginia was a second-
generation Filipino.

George Muribus of San Francisco won the San Francisco
Spelling Bee Contest at age twelve. The contest was sponsored by the San Francisco News.

April. Under the Second War Powers Act, passed on March
27, 1942, 761 Filipino ex-servicemen had become citizens
by April 7, 1946. It was announced that a total of 10,000
Filipinos had become citizens.

June 14. President Truman signed the Filipino Naturalization Bill (HR 766). Filipinos became eligible to become
United States citizens.

July 2. The Act of July 2, 1946 extended American citizenship to Filipino residents of the U.S.A. who were born in
the Philippines and who had entered the United States prior
to March 24, 1934.

August 31. The Filipino Inter-Community Organization of
America ended its eighth annual convention in San Diego.

September. The first Filipino war orphans arrived in the
United States, sponsored by the Escoda Memorial Fund.
They were Maria Theresa Escoda and her brother, Antonio,
Jr. They were to attend New York schools.

December. Mr. "Angel" (Andrew) Escalona was chosen as a member of the City Planning Board of Delano, California. He was the president of the Roxas for President Club of America.

It was announced that there were about 50,000 Filipinos in the United States.

An eleven day strike, mostly by Filipino workers, ended in Honolulu. Most of them worked on sugar plantations. They asked for higher wages.

1947 January. The Salinas Filipino Women's Club, raised $3,000 for Filipino veterans through a raffle and benefit dance.

Filipino author, Evaristo C. Pecson, received the Eugene Field Society of the National Association of Authors and Journalists Award. He was honored because of his book Our World.

February. Dr. Diosdada M. Yap, editor and publisher of Bataan magazine, prepared a "Citizenship Manual for Filipinos." It contained 500 questions and answers on United States government and the U.S. constitution. Dr. Yap was formerly on the political science faculty of Howard University.

Chicago Filipinos established another import and export enterprise. It was called the Tropical Commercial Company, with branches in New York, Tacoma, (Washington) and Manila, Philippines. Mr. Esteban Quinto was the founder.

March. Mr. Benny F. Feria compiled a book of poetry, Rhymes of My Heart. He was the editor-in-chief of the Chicago Press Service.

1948 Ms. Dalisay Aldaba made a brilliant debut as the leading singer in Madame Butterfly, with the New York City Opera Company.

January 15. Filipino veterans gathered at the Filipino Trinity Church for the purpose of organizing a new post of the American Legion for Filipino veterans in St ockton. It was named the Santo Tomas Post.

More than 200 Filipinos were attending U.S. vocational

schools under the Philippine Rehabilitation Act of 1946. Under this act, the U.S.A. authorized American agencies to spend more than $120,000,000 in training and rehabilitation projects on behalf of the Philippines.

April 14. President Manuel Roxas suddenly died of a heart attack.

July. A Filipino, Mr. A.H. Laidlaw, was appointed the owners' representative in the Orient for Pacific Transport Line, Inc. of San Francisco.

August. The Filipino Federation of America celebrated its twenty-third Annual State Convention in Stockton, California. The conference lasted eleven days.

October 6. The Supreme Court ruled in a 4 to 3 decision that California's legal ban on interracial marriage was unconstitutional. The court voided two sections of the civil code that forbade "all marriages of white persons with Negroes, Mongolians, members of the Malay race or Mulattoes."

October 15. Filipinos who had resided in the U.S.A. continuously for three years during the period ending November 30, 1941, were allowed to bring their wives and children under eighteen to the U.S.A. as "non quota immigrants." Those entering had to have a passport or immigration visa. This was stated in Part Four, Section 231 of the Philippine Trade Act of 1946, which became Public Law 371 under the Seventy-ninth Congress. The section did not apply to Hawaii.

Filipino businessman Perfecto D. Bandalan was chosen to serve as a member of a jury in a U.S. district court. This was the first time that a Filipino served on a jury in the Bay Area.

November 16. It was reported in an article by Carlos Bulosan, "The Los Angeles Police Rides Again," that detectives of the L.A. police force invaded several offices of Filipino organizations: the Manila Post 464 of the American Legion, the Labracadilla Post of the Veterans of Foreign Wars, and the Filipino Club room on Los Angeles Street. They broke furniture, smashed windows, and terrorized members and guests.

February 15. The famous war hero, Colonel J. Villamor, became an advisor to the Civil Aeronautics Administration of the U.S. government. He had resigned from the Bureau of Aeronautics of the Philippines.

February 28. More than 5,000 Filipino asparagus workers were waiting for the outcome of the present controversy between the Asparagus Growers Association and the Local 7 FTA-CIO, which had come to a deadlock in Stockton, California. There had not been a wage increase since 1942.

March 18. From Los Angeles, Vincente Villamin communicated with Representative Walter Judd, the author of a new bill on Asiatic immigration and naturalization that passed the House, to ask him that Filipinos be given an immigration quota of more than 100 a year.

May 31. In a national competition with 190 schools representing forty states, Betty Olivete, a high school student and the daughter of Mr. and Mrs. P. Olivete of Salinas, won first place honors in typing accuracy, with a record of sixty-six words per minute without errors.

June. A "Quirino for President" Club was organized in San Francisco by leaders of different Filipino communiteis on the West Coast. Mr. A. Doctolero, head of the only Filipino employment agency in northern California, was elected president.

June 30-July 4. According to a ruling by the Philippine Internal Revenue collector, Bibiano L. Meer, Filipino citizens residing in the Philippines or abroad having a gross annual income amounting to 1,000 pesos or over were required to file Philippine income tax returns on or before March 1, 1950.

August 7. Hundreds of Filipinos gathered at San Francisco International Airport to greet President E. Quirino. His entourage stayed at the Fairmount Hotel, where there were many conferences.

August 30. Adriano G. Delfino, editor of The United Filipino Press, resigned after a dispute with the publisher, Mel A. Vega. The United Filipino Press was founded in 1947 and was a unique experiment in Filipino journalism. Mr. Delfino was the night editor for the Chicago North Side news-

papers. He won the "Page One" Award with sixteen other
Chicago newspapermen.

September 30. Twenty Filipino students enrolled at Hartnell Junior College near Salinas, California.

October 27. Mr. Juan B. Sarmiento, a Filipino newspaperman and civic leader, was unanimously chosen as the "Man
of the Year for 1949" by the Manuel L. Quezon Post #603
of the American Legion. (He was also chosen by the Mail
as the "Man of the Year for 1949" on October 31.)

November 30. A Filipino center opened in Wilmington,
California. The $30,000 new center was inaugurated with
a big program.

1950   March 16. With Philippine Acting Consul General B.A. Pid-
loan as guest of honor, the Filipinos of Delano, California,
staged a "Royal Hearts Night" under the auspices of the
Filipino Women's Club in order to raise funds for the building of the Filipino Community Council of Delano.

February 22. Forty-six pensionados who had completed one
year's training with the U.S. Civil Aeronautics Administration received their diplomas at graduation ceremonies held
at the Filipino Community Center of San Francisco.

March 31. The Filipino (Philippine) consulates of Seattle,
New Orleans, Chicago, and Los Angeles were under consideration for closure for economic reasons and also because of the lack of trade promotion work.

May 15. A bill was introduced by Congressmen Teague and
Kearny that provided for burial expenses of seventy-five
dollars each for Filipino veterans. One-hundred twenty
thousand had already died, and therefore, the bill was long
overdue.

May 27. As reported in the Honolulu Star Bulletin of May 18,
agents who had been signing up unemployed Filipino laborers for California farm work faced possible prosecution for
violating a long established recruiting law.

There were more than 400 Filipino laborers who arrived in
Salinas in May. They were divided into Filipino camps.
They were either Hawaiian-born or naturalized Filipino-

Americans. It was rumored that 500 more were coming.
They were contracted for two years.

June 20. Calvin Pecson, who had just graduated from Lompoc High School, was the recipient of an alumni scholarship
for students entering the University of California at Berkeley. He was a life member of the California Scholarship
Federation. He is the son of the vice-consul general of San
Francisco.

September 3. The Roxas Club Inc. embarked on an undertaking to help those who were less fortunate to obtain an
education by running a statewide scholarship drive for
$1,500, $1,000, and $500 scholarships. Any Filipino high
school student who wished to continue his or her education
was eligible if the following qualifications were met: 1) He
or she must be a Filipino, 2) must attend a high school in
the U.S.A., and 3) must represent a Filipino community.

December 14. Under the Philippine Rehabilitation Act (Public
Law 882) passed in the Eightieth Congress, the Philippine
government sent to the United States those who sought maritime training. The first group of thirty-one ensigns graduated with four as honor students, on December 14 at the
U.S. Merchant Marine Academy at Kings Point, New York.

1951   April 16. Sam Yorty introduced a bill in the House of Representatives that would provide educational benefits to men
and women who served in the armed forces of the commonwealth of the Philippines.

July 31. The Roxas Club Inc. of Los Angeles successfully
held a popularity contest to help raise a scholarship fund
for deserving Filipino students. The winner was Ms. Am-
paro Tolentino.

September 30. The North End Filipino Growers Association
of Niland and Calipatria, the association of Filipino farmers
residing in the Imperial Valley, had a membership of eighty-
three. Most of the farmers owned their lands.

Private bills (HR 5179 and HR 5178) were introduced by Joseph Farrington that permitted Mr. and Mrs. Hilario C.
Moncado to stay in the U.S. without being subject to deportation under the Immigration and Naturalization Act.

November 23. A huge crowd went to listen to Dalisay Aldaba at the Salinas Union High School under the auspices of the Filipino community of the Salinas Valley. Ms. Aldaba was a star of the New York City Opera Company.

Consul S. Abrera of Los Angeles fought discrimination against Filipinos who had been previously permitted to be buried in certain cemeteries there. After the work of Abrera and Dr. P. Demandante, the discrimination was abolished.

1952   January. Approximately fifteen Filipino students were enrolled at Hartnell College.

April 11. The Caballero was a monthly news magazine published by the Caballeros de Dimas Alang.

May. A Filipino architect, Ariston R. Nakpil, won the second prize in the nationwide Indianapolis home show competition. He led 2160 other contestants.

July 17. Five Filipino pensionados of the Mutual Security Agency stopped in San Francisco on their way to Washington, D.C. They came to the United States to study assessment and tax collection.

December 24. The Philippine and United States governments agreed to exempt nationals from payment of visa fees when they enter as tourists, by Executive Order 535.

1953   April. A law was passed that enabled alien veterans to obtain citizenship. Honorable service in the United States armed forces might mean quick American citizenship to some alien servicemen or veterans, according to Mr. Harold W. Wildman, company service officer.

October. The United States Supreme Court declined to review the deportation case of E. Mangaoang, Local 37 International LWU business agent. It decided, in effect, that Filipinos who came to the United States prior to 1934 were undeportable. "Nationals" were not aliens. Mr. Mangaoang was accused of being affiliated with the Communist party.

1954   January. Kentuckians objected to a Filipino neighbor. Mrs. Nena Hardman, a Filipino mother of three, moved into her new home in Louisville, despite objections from some of the people who would be her neighbors.

May. Mr. Napoleon Cruz Agustin became an American citizen, through the Superior Court in San Jose, California, as a result of the law passed in 1953 that all veterans who served in the armed forces for ninety days were eligible to become naturalized citizens of the United States of America.

December. Jack B. Wright, a former Salinas police officer, was named a defendant in a $15,000 false imprisonment suit filed in superior court in Salinas by P.B. Espejo, operator of a restaurant, who was arrested on October 31.

1955   July. Pursuing its planned merchandising program to serve rural areas in California and other parts of the Union, Associated Stores, Inc., a mail-order discount house recently organized by Filipinos and Americans, placed on the market a natural soil conditioner and fertilizer trade-named Agricol. It is mixed in Nevada, and it influences plant growth.

October. The Filipino community of Salinas Valley, California, held a banquet and ball in connection with the community building fund drive. Senator Fred Farr was a guest speaker. The senator told his audience about a bill that had been approved by the state legislature for the benefit of alien residents.

Mr. Miguel, a farmer at Milpitas, California, won a prize for his first crop of tobacco leaves at the Santa Clara County Fair. It was the first time such an entry was presented. The tobacco seeds were from the Philippines.

November. General Hilario C. Moncado, founder of the Filipino Federation of America, became a resident of Baja California in Mexico.

1956   January 8. The Filipino United Community Organization was formed in San Jose, California. The purpose was to work for the general welfare of the Filipinos and their families whether they were citizens of the United States or the Philippines. Ms. Maxine Gonong was elected its first president.

March 11. Mayor Alva Andrus and Supervisor B.L. Talcott, represented the city and county, respectively, at the ground breaking of the site of the Filipino Community Hall and Center in Salinas, California.

July 8. In memory of the late General H.C. Moncado, founder of the Filipino Federation of America, a banquet was held at the Stockton Hotel, Stockton, California. It was attended by city officials and many Filipino leaders.

August. Negotiations were rounded out for the transportation of 10,000 Filipinos to work on Pacific Coast farms. Nick Roxas, consul, was discussing the situation as immigration laws were being studied.

October 14. A group of Filipino labor contractors and leaders in the Salinas Valley and Watsonville, California, met at the Dimas Alang Temple for the purpose of forming an organization in the interest of both the farm industry and field labor. The organization was called the Farm Labor Service Association. One of the aims of the organization was to urge farm growers, shippers, and farmers to recruit labor from the Philippines and another was to alleviate Filipino unemployment.

November. Pedro Padilla arrived in San Francisco as a personal representative of President R. Magsaysay to conduct negotiations with the California Growers Association on the importation of laborers to work on farms on a contractual basis. Mr. Padilla was a well-known Filipino newspaperman.

1957

January. Miss Monica Gorospe was chosen Miss Filipino-America of 1956-1957 at a dance sponsored by the Filipino American Post, No. 652.

Filipino-American leaders honored Governor Rossellini of Washington with a luncheon at the new Washington Hotel in Seattle under the auspices of the Filipino-American Citizens League. A program of short talks and an open discussion about problems affecting the Filipino-Americans residing in Washington followed the luncheon. (The preceding governors of Washington had refused to give audience to Filipinos.)

March 1. It was reported that the first group of 70 Filipinos, out of 1,000 who were permitted to come to California under the terms of a "new treaty" between the United States and the Philippines, was due to arrive in San Francisco.

Thomas Rubio was elected president of the Filipino Community of Imperial Valley, California.

The Filipino community of Yuma, Arizona, donated $300 to the March of Dimes drive and also donated $100 to the Community Chest.

March 12-13. Salvador del Fierro, Sr., foreman at Ketchikan's Sunny Point Cannery Plant, was one of the judges during the nineteenth Annual Canned Salmon Cutting Demonstration at the Olympic Hotel in Seattle, Washington. He was the first and only Filipino foreman in Alaska to participate in the canned salmon cutting demonstration.

May. Cicilio Martinez, Jr., a resident of Hotville, California was the recipient of a scholarship award from the Future Farmers of America.

June 25. Cannery workers of the International Longshoremen's and Warehousemen's Union Local No. 37 of Seattle, Washington, made an aggregated gain of about $60,000.00 over the 1956 wages in the recently negotiated contract with the canned salmon industry, according to Gene Navarro, business agent. The company agreed to recognize Local No. 37 as the sole and exclusive bargaining agent of all employees hired from California, Oregon, and Washington.

July. Teresita Salvosa Requiro, a valedictorian of the class of 1957 of Carmel High School, Carmel, California, was the first Filipina to graduate as a valedictorian in a public high school in the United States.

July. The Yulo for President Club was organized in San Francisco, with its headquarters at the Soriano Building. The purpose of the club was to help elect Mr. Jose Yulo for president in the November national election in the Philippines.

August. Mr. E. Victoria Bacho, selected by the Mail in August, 1956 as one of the ten leading citizens of the Pacific Northwest, graduated with a Bachelor of Arts degree in political science at the University of Washington.

Dr. Primitva Demandante, the only Filipina practicing physician and surgeon in Wilmington, California, was installed as president of the American Women's Association. She owned her medical building, was one of two practicing Filipina doctors in the United States, and was on the Seaside Hospital staff in Long Beach, California. The continuous project of the association was the raising of scholarship funds for worthy women medical students.

September 17. Mr. Mariano B. Angeles of Seattle, Washington, was the recipient of a United States Post Office Department certificate of award signed by Postmaster General Arthur E. Summerfield and countersigned by S.G. Schwartz, regional director. The certificate of award served as an official commendation and appreciation for contributing a beneficial suggestion to the postal service of the United States.

A $50 prize was awarded to the Filipino community float of Wapato, Washington. It scored first place in the parade of floats at the city's annual Labor Day Harvest Festival.

October. Filipino citizens residing permanently in the Territory of Hawaii were strongly urged by the Philippine consul general, Juan C. Dionisio, to file their applications as soon as possible if they were thinking about bringing to the territory their spouse or minor children.

The eighth biennial convention of the Legionarios del Trabajo in America, one of three major Filipino fraternal organizations in the continental United States, was held in San Jose, California.

1958   January 18-26. Over 300 delegates representing seventy-one lodges for Hawaii, Alaska, and the United States attended the fifteenth Triennial Convention of the Caballeros de Dimas Alang, Inc. in Seattle, Washington.

May. Maximo Jose Callao was the recipient of a $200 scholarship to Hartnell College from the Filipino Women's Club of Salinas.

July 15. Barbara Olinio, winner of the 1958 California Intermediate Ladies Roller Skating Championship held at Garden Grove, left for Washington, D.C. to represent the state of California in the national championship.

November 30. Pauline Dominisa, employed as a houseboy for twenty years by a wealthy Philadelphia family, received $200,000.00 from the family estate.

1959   February. The University of Washington alumni in Honolulu, Hawaii, named Philippine Consul General Juan C. Dionisio as "distinguished alumnus." He graduated from the Seattle university in 1936.

The Seattle Filipino Knights of Columbus spearheaded a drive to raise money as a gift to the St. Thomas Seminary. They presented a check of $475 to Archbishop Thomas A. Connolly.

August 15. The first edition of The Filipino-American News was published by Catuiva and Associated, Inc., whose offices are in San Francisco, California, Los Angeles, and San Diego. James Catuiva is president of the company.

1960   April. Free X-rays were offered to Filipino residents in the San Francisco area. "Tuberculosis killed two Filipinos in 1959 and struck 24 others," said Dr. Fred Blake, a Tuberculosis Association spokesman. Dr. Blake estimated that fifty Filipinos living in San Francisco had TB but didn't realize it.

Philip A. Sun, son of Mr. and Mrs. F. Sun of Salinas, California, was the twelfth recipient of the $200 scholarship that the Filipino Women's Club awards to deserving senior students of Filipino descent.

June 30. George R. Pena, an employee of the State Division of Real Estate, California Department of Investment, achieved the distinction of having won the greatest number of citations from the State Merit Award Board with a total of seven awards and five certificates of commendation.

The Filipino adult class sponsored by the Filipino-American Catholic Association, duly recognized by the Salinas Adult School, ended its 1959-1960 term. Citizenship and English for the foreign-born were taugh by Mrs. Josefina A. Cadiz, a fully accredited Salinas school teacher.

1961   January 21. Former United States Army Captain Lescum de la Cruz was reelected commander of the "American Prisoners of War" in an election held at Fort Lawton's Officers' Club in Seattle.

February. Celestino Alfafara, grand master of the Caballeros de Dimas Alang for the previous twelve years, was organizing a "Jose Rizal Centennial Tour" under the auspices of the Philippine American Travel Agency in San Francisco. A tourist guide would lead the pilgraimage to the birthplace of Jose Rizal and then to his grave.

July. The Cannery Worker's Union Local 37 of the ILWU in Seattle only sent 500 men to Alaska this season. This figure represented the biggest cutback of Filipino workers during its existence. More than 4,000 men used to man the operation in the salmon canneries more than twenty years ago. The union was undergoing a financial crisis.

October. The Pangasinan Association of Central California was formed in Santa Rita, California. Mr. and Mrs. Alex Barnachia spearheaded the formation of the association.

October 2. Santiago Beltran, Jr., believed to be the first Filipino ever to join Seattle's police force, was sworn in.

1961   November 16-19. The Legionarios del Trabajo celebrated their tenth biennial convention in Los Angeles at the Biltmore Hotel.

1962   February. Prudencio Mori, an executive council member of the Seattle Filipino Community, Inc., was one of the panel speakers on "Oriental Communities in Seattle." Mr. Mori stated that there were over 3,000 Filipino residents in the city.

April 30. California became the first state in the nation to extend disability insurance to agricultural workers. Workers who had suffered disability injuries or illnesses not connected with their job might file disability claims. Farm workers had to have received $300.00 in wages during the three month period ending the previous December 31 in order to be eligible for benefits filed in May, June, and July. Disability benefits ranged from $10.00 to $70.00 a week, depending on how much was earned.

September 30. Consul General Holigares succeeded in getting pledges of support from no less than forty Filipino organization heads and civic leaders in a plan to organize themselves into an intercommunity council.

December. A total of $250.00 was raised by Filipinos in Washington, D.C., as their initial contribution to the fund for those of their countrymen who were hit recently by a severe typhoon in Guam.

1963   January 31. Caballeros de Dimas Alang held a successful conference in Stockton.

February 23. Captain Lescum de la Cruz, president of the
Filipino American Inter-Community of the Pacific Northwest,
was again chosen a member of the Speakers Bureau of the
Seattle Chamber of Commerce.

March 23. The Filipino-American Inter-Community Council
of the Pacific Northwest held its quarterly conference. Current problems and reports of prime importance were discussed and made during the conference.

April 27. Dominador C. Manuel, president of the Filipino
Community of Salinas Valley, Inc. for the previous six years,
died. He was a labor contractor for the Bruce Church Company for fifteen years and a field foreman of the same company for the last five years.

May 11. Mrs. Florencio Tugade was named Mother and Woman of the Year on Mother's Day by the Women's Society
of Christian Service of the Seattle Filipino Fellowship Me-
thodist Church.

1964   January. The Filipino-American Inter-Pacific Council of
the Pacific Northwest reelected Captain Lescum de la Cruz
as its president at its annual convention held in Wapato,
Washington.

March 12. Mr. Mariano B. Masilongan, former editor of
The Philippines Mail and a resident of Salinas for about
thirty years, died.

April. Valentin Osias Arellano, a labor contractor, was
elected city councilman of Gonzales, California. He was the
first Philippine-born naturalized American citizen in Monterey County to win an elective office and the second in
California to serve as councilman. (The first was Alex Alcantara, Jr., elected city councilman of Soledad a few years
previously.)

June 21. Captain Lescum de la Cruz, an outstanding leader
of the Filipino community, was chosen Man of the Year during an annual dinner of the ex-prisoners of war held at Seattle's Fort Lawton Officer's Club.

July. A clinic was opened by Mr. Mauricio Origenes, a li-
censed physician, close to the Children's Orthopedic Hospital in Seattle, Washington.

October. It was the thirty-fourth anniversary of The Philippines Mail.

October 3. President Diosdado Macapagal of the Philippines began a twelve-day visit to the United States. He was honored with a banquet and ball by the Filipino Council of Northern and Central California on October 11 at the Hilton Hotel.

December. It was reported that Filipino servicemen who joined the U.S. armed forces following the liberation of the Philippines in World War II were now eligible for United States citizenship.

1965   January. Brock Adams, newly-elected Congressman for King County's seventh district of Seattle, Washington, praised the Filipino's support for him in his bid for office.

February 5-6. Filipino students, folk singers, and dancers participated in the International Show at Edmund Meany's auditorium of the University of Washington.

March. Florentino L. Gamboa, a local businessman and civic leader, won the distinction of being the first Filipino to run for councilman in the city of San Jose, California.

March 20. Filipinos of Yakima Valley, Washington, observed the thirteenth anniversary of their $50,000.00 clubhouse hall. A program of speeches, Philippine folk dances, and native songs followed a sumptuous dinner. Philippine Consul General Eotola R. Sulit was a guest speaker.

May. It was reported that Rep. Charles S. Gubser (R-Cal) introduced a bill in Congress to admit aliens willing to work at least two years on American farms. All those admitted had to be close relatives of United States residents. After two years of farm work, the immigrant could remain in the United States as a permanent resident.

August 7. Seattle's Filipino Nurses' Association held its picnic at Seward Park. The picnic included a business meeting presided by Mrs. B. Sison, vice-president of the group.

August 10. Filipinos in Salinas, California, hosted the world-famous Filipino Youth Activities of Seattle's colorful Cumbanchero Drill Team and Mandayan Marchers, who performed at the Hartnell College gymnasium.

September. Seattle Filipinos finally got a clubhouse, and
President Urbano Quijance of the Filipino Community Council gave the finishing touches to a building costing $80,000.
The clubhouse project had been started over thirty-eight
years earlier by donations of Filipino workers in the salmon
canneries of Alaska.

President Lyndon B. Johnson signed a new immigration law
at the foot of the Statue of Liberty. The national origin quota
system, which was first instituted in 1924, would be abolished
under this new law, effective July, 1968. In its place would
be a world quota set at 270,000, out of which 120,000 would
be allotted to Canada and the Latin countries. Under the law,
spouses and minor children and parents of United States
citizens were to be admitted outside the quotas without nu-
merical limitation.

October. The first available Tagalog textbook was published
by the University of California Press. Beginning Tagalog:
A Course for Speakers of English, is a one-year course for
adult speakers of English. It was a joint effort of the Philippine Center for Language Study, under the auspices of the
Bureau of Public Schools of the Republic of the Philippines,
and the Department of English, University of California at
Los Angeles. Tagalog is used by an estimated 13 million
people.

November. Under the leadership of Emile Heredia of the
Philippine-American Travel Agency of San Francisco, a
dozen Filipino-Americans met and organized the Filipino-
American Political Association (FAPA). The principla office
was in San Francisco but its work would cover all of California. The purpose was a) to promote interest and unite all
groups and individuals engaged in work aimed at raising the
economy, welfare, education, and social level of Filipino-
Americans; b) to foster and promote community-wide interest and concern for problems of Filipino-Americans, to end
discrimination, economic and otherwise; and c) to investigate,
research, and study the problems of the Filipino-American
community and to furnish reports thereon to the various
groups and agencies concerned therewith.

1966   January 8. The Marcos-Lopez Club, organized by Mr. M.R.
Galicia, Sr., held a victory banquet and ball in honor of the
election of Ferdinand Marcos and Fernando Lopez, president
and vice-president, respectively.

July. The Filipino-American Political Association instituted a survey among all Filipino-American organizations in northern California seeking to obtain some insight into the position of Filipino-Americans on matters of current political interest. President Heredia said that the FAPA would take an active part in forthcoming campaigns and for that reason the plight of the Filipino-Americans in all social and economic areas would be of paramount concern in selecting candidates for endorsement.

September 24. Ferdinand Marcos, president of the Republic of the Philippines, was guest of honor at a banquet given by the Filipino-American Council of Northern California at the Fairmount Hotel in San Francisco. Governor E. Brown and Mayor Shelley were also guest speakers.

December. The Gran Oriente Filipino, one of the most solvent fraternal organizations in the United States, held its annual convention in Seattle.

1967   January. Veterans benefits for Filipino citizens who served the United States armed forces in World War II were liberalized in certain respects: payments were tied to the dollar instead of the peso and educations for war orphans was extended to children of Filipino veterans who served with the U.S. forces, at $.50 on the dollar.

January 16-22. The eighteenth triennial convention of the CDA (Caballeros de Dimas Alang) was held in Stockton, California. Five men proclaimed their candidacy for grand master: Jose Reyes of Los Angeles, E. Vic Bacho of Seattle, Max Peralta of San Jose, Cosme Brasil of Los Angeles, and Pablo Parocha of Stockton.

January 29. Seattle's Filipino Youth Activities feted its tenth anniversary at the City's Central Olympic Room. Fred Cordova, moderator, director, and founder, acted as master. More than 200 attended.

March. Dr. D.B. Ines ran for the Florida State House of Representatives. In the previous election, Dr. Ines had been a candidate for state representative. He was one of the first Filipinos who ran for high public office. He is well-known and was included in the latest Who's Who in Florida.

June 3. Fernando Lopez, twice vice-president of the Philip-

pines, was honored at a dinner and dance reception at the
Grand Ballroom of the Fairmount Hotel in San Francisco.
Several Filipino organizations sponsored the event.

1968   March 10. Seattle Filipinos attended a meeting at the Filipino Community Center to hear about taxation covering income tax to the government of the Philippines. Commonwealth Act 466 stated: "All Filipinos of 18 years of age and
above residing in the Philippines and overseas, earning a
yearly gross income of 1,800 pesos ($461.00) must file their
income tax return with the Bureau of Internal Revenue."
Tax evasion meant imprisonment and fine or both.

July. Dr. Max Rafferty, superintendant of public insturction
and of the Department of Education of the State of California,
stated that any teacher from the Philippines who had the
equivalent of a United States BA could be certified to teach
in California. But the primary problem was that most Philippine teachers who came to California had the equivalent of
only two years of United States education.

July 28. Consul R.M. Balias of San Francisco supported the
cause of Filipino dentists in California before the California
Board of Dental Examiners. Dentists from the Philippines
were not allowed to take the dental board exams in order
to practice in California. The requirements were so stiff
that even Filipinos finishing their studies in the leading universities in the Philippines could not qualify. This included
Filipinos either naturalized or permanent residents of the
Unived States. Senate Bill 215 and Assembly Bill 1934 were
written to support the efforts made for those frustrated Filipino dentists. A committee was created to investigate and
iron out whatever differences or deficiencies foreign dentists
might have had in order to make it possible for them to be
admitted to practice in California.

October. More than 250 people attended the annual convention for the Filipino Catholic Association held at the John
Kennedy Youth Center in Watsonville, California.

November. Leo de Leon began his fifth term as president
of the Filipino-American Community of Puget Sound, Inc.

December. A sixty-eight-page anniversary book was well
received by Seattle Filipinos. It was dedicated to Filipino
pioneers who started the $80,000 Filipino Community of Se-

attle Inc. social center. The publication was edited by Julius
B. Ruiz. E. Vic Bacho was the publisher and editorial board
chairman. The book covered the history of Filipinos in Seattle and the Pacific Northwest.

F.A. Gonzales of Salinas was elected chairman of the Board
of Governors of Serra International. He presided over the
meeting of governors of Serra Clubs comprising the districts
of Northern California and Nevada. Serra International is
composed of 350 clubs around the world whose members
are select Catholic laymen for the work of vocations.

1969   January. F.A. Ribultan joined The Philippines Mail. He was
            a graduate of Cabrillo College in the Santa Cruz County.

            March. Elisa Nerez of Salinas, California, was declared
            state winner of an essay contest conducted by the National
            Employ (sic) the Handicapped. She was a senior student at
            Alisal High School.

            Who's Who in America, Inc., announced that the Philippine
            consul general for San Francisco, Samson Sabalones, had
            been selected as a Biographer in volume 36 of Who's Who
            in America.

            March 28-30. The Filipino-American Political Association
            of California (FAPA) held its annual state convention.

            May. All Filipino teachers teaching in California were urged
            to join the newly organized Filipino Teachers' Association
            with headquarters in San Francisco.

            May 30. Dr. Bernado Acena was named "an outstanding
            alumnus" and Edward Fontecha Tajon was named a scholar
            at the annual banquet and ball honoring Filipino-American
            high school graduates in Washington State.

            June 12. The celebrated AB537, known as the Filipino Dental
            Bill, was signed into law by Governor Ronald Reagan of Cali-
            fornia. The law would allow Filipino dentists to practice
            their profession in the State of California.

            June. Six Filipino organizations in Salinas Valley awarded
            scholarships to Filipino-American honor students.

            August. Tagalog, the national language of the Philippines,

was scheduled to be taught in San Francisco as part of the
bilingual education program. A total of $9,965 was allocated
for the program as a result of the proposal submitted by
Silvestre Santos.

September. Three Filipino-Americans of the 1969 Alisal
High School graduating class were awarded college opportunity grants to attend Hartnell College.

October. Dr. Manuel S. Tustior joined the Department of
Economics and Business of the University of Washington in
the fall quarter of 1969.

December. Mrs. Tiburcio V. Mejia was crowned Queen of
the Filipino Community of Seattle for 1970.

1970   May 8. Governor Reagan of California appointed a Filipino
judge for Los Angeles. Miss Marion Lacadia Obera became
the first judge of Filipino ancestry to sit on a judicial bench
in the continental United States.

May. Construction began on the Filipino Cultural Center of
San Luis Obispo.

July. Alaskan cannery workers got a thirty-five dollar
monthly increase by the efforts of the International Longshoremen's and Warehousemen's Union Local No. 7.

October. Dr. F.A. Gonzales, a noted local Filipino physician and surgeon of Salinas, California, was one of the few,
if not the only, Filipino listed in Who's Who in America.

1971   March. Abbott Laboratories, one of the biggest pharmaceu-
tical companies in this country, gave F.A. Gonzales, M.D.,
of Salinas a research grant to evaluate a new psychotropic
drug.

April. The Seattle Executive Department's Youth Division
awarded a grant to Filipino Youth Activites of Seattle. The
grant was to be used for expanded cultural enrichment programs and student job opportunities.

June. The Juan V. Mina Farms in the Puyallup Valley, Washington, operated acres of strawberry patches. Mr. Mina is
known as the "Strawberry King" of that part of the valley.

December. Ernest Escutron won $12,000 in scholarships. Ernest, a resident of San Francisco, California, won a 10,000 scholarship from the National Maritime Union and also a $2,000 scholarship for being the most outstanding American high school student.

1972   January. Dion V. Corsilles, the managing editor of Todd News, was one of the five winners of the Orchid Award given by the Pacific Northwest Industrial editors at a conference held at the Seattle-Tacoma Hilton.

January 19. The former Philippine ambassador to Portugal, Estela Romualdez Sulit, who made Seattle her home, died of a heart attack in Seattle at the age of seventy.

March. The meeting to discuss the impact of the hotel closure in the Seattle International District was held at the International Drop-In Center in Seattle. Approximately 175 Filipinos were faced with the problem of relocation due to the planned closure.

March 25. The Filipino-American Council named four council representatives in Washington State to serve on Governor Daniel Evans's advisory board. One member would be named by Evans to serve as a representative on minority ethnic groups. Members were Jose Prudencio, Vincent Barrios, Tony Baruso, and Juanito Umipig.

July. A new organization composed mostly of professionals and civic leaders from the Western Visayas was organized at the residence of Mr. and Mrs. A. Reyes in Monterey Park, California. The organization was called the Greater Hiligaynon of Southern California.

July 5. The Washington State Council on Aging approved the International Drop-In Center's application for a project grant totaling $25,370.

September 28-29. A national organization of United States Filipino-American citizens was established in a conference at Seattle's Sorrento Hotel. Professor Manuel S. Rustia was named general chairman.

October. Dr. Dulzura was invited to be a speaker at the International Minority Business Seminar that was held at the Lost Angeles Convention Center. He was president of the Filipino-American Community of Los Angeles, California, Inc.

November 18. Mrs. Joan Mendoza Kis was named the 1972
Mrs. Filipino Community at the final contest held at the
Seattle Filipino Community Center.

December 15. It was reported by the Filipino-American
Herald that Filipino Youth Activites, Inc. was awarded $300
by IBM for their youth camping program.

Vincent F. Flor, an employee of the Pacific Marine Center's
processing division, received a special achievement certificate from Norman E. Taylor, the center's director.

1973   January 7. Silvestre A. Tangalan was re-elected president
of the Filipino Community of Seattle, Inc.

Assemblyman Willie L. Brown, Jr., announced the signing
into law of his bill that enable foreign-trained pharmacists
to practice their profession in California without completing
courses in the United States. He was quoted as saying that
he introduced the bill due to his concern for highly experi-
enced Filipinos who were forced to return to school in order
to obtain a license to practice in California.

February 9. Julius B. Ruiz, Filipino-American Herald's
contributing editor of Seattle, died of a heart attack at the
age of sixty-five.

February 18-25. Seattle Mayor Wes Uhlman proclaimed
February 18-25 Filipino Youth Week in the City of Seattle.

March. The American College of Cardiology at its annual
convention in San Francisco presented its highest award,
given annually to one cardiologist, to Dr. M. Alimurung,
a prominent Filipino cardiologist from Manila. (Dr. Alimurung was the first non-American to be honored.) He was
the founding president of the Philippine Heart Association.

Foreign Secretary Carlos Romulo arrived for two weeks of
talks with business and tour groups to tell them more about
the Philippines of 1973. "People in the United States" he
said, "are very much interested in the new Society in the
Philippines and want to hear about it." He said a new confi-
dence in the Philippines was developing abroad.

April 12. Jack Anderson's column in the Seattle Post-Intelli-
gencer stated that there were approximately 120 Filipino

stewards stationed in the Washington, D.C., area. Of these, thirty-two were assigned to Headquarters, Naval District, Washington. Another fifty-eight are assigned to the Navy Administration Unit, which is the official designation for those stewards to the White House staff.

April 16. It was reported that the Filipino Community Council decided to establish a community blood bank. The goal was to establish 200 units in the community blood bank.

Edwin Almerol was in Salinas interviewing old-timer Filipinos. He hoped to improve the knowledge of Filipino-Americans in the United States. He was a doctoral candidate in anthropology at the University of Illinois and chose Salinas for his study because of the long, established history of the Filipino community there.

The Department of Justice of the Philippines, in response to an inquiry by the embassy of Washingto, D.C., stated that Filipino-Americans who own land in the Philippines may legally continue to own it. However, according to both the 1935 Philippine Constitution and the new constitution (which went into effect in January, 1973), these lands "may be transferred or conveyed only to citizens of the Philippines or to corporations or associations at least 60 percent of the capital of which is owned by such citizens, save in cases of hereditary succession."

Philippine citizens across the United States were unduly jarred by the news of Marcos's Presidential Decree No. 174, which stated that they have to pay their taxes to his government on a flat percentage of total income earned. Filipinos residing outside of the Philippines who had a net taxable income of more than $13,000 in 1971 and prior years could take advantage of the new decree by filing the corresponding return and paying 10 percent of any excess over the $13,000.

The first Filipino-American commercial bank in the United States opened in Los Angeles, California. The bank, International Bank of California, was the first and only bank in the United States that involved Filipinos in its management and control. Four Filipino-Americans were serving on the board: Dr. B. Tan, A. Holigores, J. Licuanan, and Dr. R. Navarro.

May. Filipinos abroad who were holding or hoarding Philippine currency were advised to exchange it for new currency.

Otherwise, after 1973, when the demonetization took place, the money would become useless.

The Philippine Consul General in San Francisco announced that on the basis of information and instructions received, all Filipino citizens residing in the United States who desired to go to the Philippines might do so, and their return to the United States would be guaranteed.

May 15. It was reported by Gene Navarro that the closure of at least nine canneries by operators of the Alaska salmon industry would put many Filipinos out of work.

July. Philippine Cultural Foundation of Santa Clara, Cal., Inc. was incorporated. The purpose of the only Philippine cultural center in California was charitable and educational.

July 16. Nemesio Domingo was named Father of the Year for the Filipino Community of Seattle.

August. Twelve Filipino generals were included in the new Allied Officer Hall of Fame at the United States Army Command and General Staff College at Fort Leavenworth, Kansas. The hall of fame displayed graduates of the United States Army's top professional schools.

October. President Ferdinand Marcos approved dual citizenship for natural-born Filipinos who have acquired American citizenship. (It was intended to enable older Filipino-Americans who retired in the Philippines to acquire land and enjoy rights as any other citizen.

November 26. Lamberto Aledia, a Filipino sailor in the United States Navy, won a one-million-dollar prize in the Massachusetts State Lottery.

Balikbayan was announced by Marcos, which is an open invitation to all overseas Filipinos to visit the Philippines. A special low-rate tour was offered.

1974   January 21-26. The Caballeros de Dimas Alang, Inc. held a conference at the San Francisco Sheraton Palace Hotel for all members in the United States and Hawaii. Three hundred to four hundred members attended.

February. Casino Cafe, the oldest Philippine restaurant in

Seattle, established in February, 1949, celebrated its twenty-fifth anniversary. The proprietor was Mr. Ignacio Navarette.

February. Max Callao of Boise, Idaho, was promoted to the rank of associate professor of Psychology at Boise State College. In 1973 he was recognized in the twelfth edition of American Men and Women of Science: The Social and Behavioral Sciences.

A Filipino architect, Richard Galvez, was appointed to the planning commission of Fremont, California. He is the architect of the proposed ten-acre cultural park of the Cultural Center projects of the Filipino Community of Santa Clara.

March. The Philippines were second, after Mexico, in number of immigrants to the United States, with 25,696 for the year of 1973. So far, 35,000 Filipinos have returned to the Philippines for visits.

April. Juneau's three hundred Alaskan-Filipinos were praised by officials upon the occasion of the National Bank of Alaska's loan of $40,000 to build the new Filipino Community Center.

A Hawaiian of Filipino ancestry was named to the Hawaii Supreme Court. He was Ben Banoy, the elder brother of State Representative Barney Banoy.

June 8. The Filipino War Brides Association of Seattle celebrated its twenty-fifth anniversary. Mr. Mariano Angeles, founder of the association, was the guest speaker.

August. A Filipino-American Association was organized on the naval base at Lemore, California, with eighty families.

September 30. About 7,000 Filipino teachers registered with the U.S. embassy were not given immigration visas to enter the United States because there were too many teachers already.

October 1. Fred and Dorothy Cordova, founder of Filipino Youth Activities of Seattle, Inc., were presented with the Wing Luke Award for 1972. The annual award is presented by the Seattle-King County Youth Commission but had not been presented for three years due to reorganization.

October 4. Luis Taruc, former leader of the Hukbalahap (Communists), lectured at the University of Washington in Seattle. His lecture was cosponsored by the Filipino Youth Activities, Inc. and the University of Washington Institute for Comparative and Foreign Area Studies.

Mr. Macario Regaspi of Los Angeles, California, was indicted by a federal grand jury and subsequently convicted of assaulting a United States border patrolman with a shotgun. At the trial, the border patrolman said he stopped Regaspi's vehicle because it was weaving dangerously. Regaspi's attorney, G.G. Manibog, told the court that Mr. Regaspi was driving in a normal manner and that the border patrolman merely wanted a pretext to make an improper immigration check (recently held by the United States Supreme Court to be unconstitutional when conducted away from international borders).

DOCUMENTS

CONSTITUTION OF THE "KNIGHTS OF RIZAL"
1906

The following document was adopted by Filipino students who attended the Filipino Students' Convention that was held at Cobb Hall, University of Chicago, during the first week of September, 1906. Although it is not clear who these students were, the University of Chicago had a number of pensionados who came to the United States to study at the government's expense.

Source: The Filipino Students' Magazine, Vol. II, No. 3, October 1906.

Article I. -- Name.

We, the undersigned, under oath, hereby do constitute and organize a fraternal order, hereafter to be known as "Knights of Rizal."

Article II. -- Purposes.

The purposes of this order are: fraternity, mutual help and protection among the members, and the promotion of the best interests and general welfare of the Filipino people.

Article III. -- Organization.

1. The order shall consist of the main council, which will hereafter be known as "The Trunk," to be established in no definite place, and such other sub-councils as may be necessary to be formed to be hereafter known as "Branches."

2. The officers of the trunk will consist of:

(a) A Supreme Regulator.
(b) A Deputy Supreme Regulator.
(c) A General Keeper of the Archives.
(d) A General Head of Finances.
(e) A General Guardian Knight.

3. The officers of the branches will consist of:

(a) A Regulator.
(b) A Deputy Regulator.
(c) A Keeper of the Archives.
(d) A Head of Finances.
(e) A Guardian Knight.

4. A branch may be established in any place where there are at least five Filipino students, on application to the trunk.

Article IV. -- Meetings.

1. Two-thirds of the members of the trunk or any branch, shall constitute a quorum.

2. General - A general meeting will be held annually by the members of the association at an appointed time and place. However, if all the members cannot attend personally for a justifiable reason they may send a delegate or delegates to the aforesaid general meeting. . . .

3. Local - The trunk and the branches will hold local meetings on every first and third Sunday of each month.

4. All meetings of this order shall be held secretly.

Article V. -- Entrance and Expulsion of Members.

1. Any Filipino student in America or in the Philippine Islands born in the Islands recommended by two members of good standing, may be admitted by vote of at least all but two of the members present at the branch meeting wherein the admission is sought.

2. Any of the following shall be a sufficient cause for the expulsion of any member from the order:

(a) Non-payment of dues for the period of three months.
(b) Any conduct unbecoming a gentleman and a true Filipino.
(c) Any divulgation of the secret affairs of this order.

Article VI. -- Fees.

1. The entrance fee of this order shall be one dollar.

2. The monthly fee shall be twenty-five cents.

Article VII. -- Election and Impeachment of Officers.

1. The election of officers shall be by the majority of the members at the election.

2. A majority of the members present at the trial shall be necessary to impeach an officer.

3. Any of the following shall be sufficient cause for impeachment of any officer:

(a) Any cause sufficient to expel a member from this order.
(b) Any negligence of official duty or duties.

Article VII. -- Duties and Powers of Officers.

1. The Supreme Regulator. - The Supreme Regulator shall:

(a) Preside over all general meetings and over those of the trunk.
(b) Execute the orders, resolutions and by laws of the order.
(c) Adjudge the elections of the general officers.
(d) Call special meetings of the trunk and branches.
(e) Preside over impeachment trials of any general officers except himself.
(f) Supervise and regulate the different branch officers.

2. The Deputy Supreme Regulator. - The Deputy Supreme Regulator shall:

    (a) Fill the place of the Supreme Regulator in case of absence, sickness or death during his term of office or removal by impeachment.

3. The General Keeper of the Archives. - The General Keeper of the Archives shall:

    (a) Keep an accurate record:
        (1) Of the proceedings in the meetings of the trunk.
        (2) Of the proceedings in the general meetings.
    (b) Receive and send all communications necessary pertaining to the business of the order.

4. The General Head of Finances. - The General Head of Finances shall:

    (a) Receive and dispurse the funds of the order with the proper supervision of the Supreme Regulator.
    (b) Keep accurate records of the funds of the order.
    (c) Hold the funds at hand of the order.
    (d) Give proper securities.

5. The General Guardian Knight. - The General Guardian Knight shall:

    (a) Keep order in the general meeting and of those of the trunk.
    (b) Execute the orders of the Supreme Regulator.

Article IX. -- Relation Between the Trunk and Branches.

1. The Trunk has a general control of the affairs affecting two or more branches.

2. The Branches will have the power to regulate over their own local affairs.

3. The Branches are bound to send to the General Head of Finance ten cents for each actual member monthly and fifty cents of the entrance fee.

Article X. -- Amendments.

1. Two-thirds of the members present in a general meeting may amend any provision or provisions of this constitution.

2. The next Filipino Students' Convention in the Middle West should be held during the last week of next December, 1906, in Chicago, Ill.

3. The next anniversary of the death of our most beloved patriot, Rizal, should be commemorated by the members of the convention of the 30th of next December, 1906, in Chicago, Ill.

4. Election of a committee to request the editors of the Filipino Students' Magazine and the Filipino to create a review in the magazines

they publish, in order to remedy the wrong ideas that the Americans have about the Filipinos, and to present before the eyes of the American public the true condition of affairs in the Philippines.

5. Rectification by the convention of a false statement that appeared in the edition of the "Chicago Examiner," September the 5th, against the opinions of its members, on account of the fact that in the edition of the "Chicago Examiner," September the 5th, appeared a statement saying: "That the members of the convention realize that the Filipinos are not capable of self-government." And being a fact that such a statement did not come from their opinions, it was resolved by the convention that a committee be appointed to interview with the editor of same newspaper in order to rectify the above statement.

6. The convention shall not be partial to either one of the two magazines (The Filipino Students' Magazine and The Filipino), published by the Filipino students in America.

Regarding the new organization, "Knights of Rizal," the attention of my fellow-students may be called upon to the fact that its "constitution" is subject to changes. It gives to the members a right to amend any provision or provisions of such a "constitution," as provided in Article X. It requires courage that the Filipino students in the Middle West be gathered in a place only for the purpose of getting more together in their feelings, in their needs and in their ideals. That they have realized an important work in the early past it is beyond any doubt; that they may obtain a more fruitful result in their efforts and cooperation of their fellow-students in the East, as well as in the West. It is for a great realization, therefore that every Filipino student in this country, at least, should join this new movement, make it a great organization and lead it to a true success.

ARTICLES OF INCORPORATION OF THE FILIPINO
FEDERATION OF AMERICA
1927

As one of the first social organizations for Filipinos in America, the Filipino Federation of America has contributed to enhancement of the Filipinos' interest by standing for their rights. The organization fought for Filipinos in their struggle for American citizenship. Dr. Hilario Camino Moncado was one of the most respected Filipinos in America.

Source: Exclusion of Immigration from the Philippine Islands. Hearings before the Committee on Immigration and Naturalization, House of Representatives. 71st Congress, Second Session. U.S. Government Printing Office, 1930.

Know all men by these presents, that we, the undersigned, a majority of whom are citizens and residents of the State of California, do hereby voluntarily associate ourselves together for the purpose of incorporating under the laws of the State of California a private corporation.

And we do hereby certify:

First.   The name of said corporation shall be Filipino Federation of America.

Second.   That the purposes for which said corporation is formed are:

(a) To promote friendly relations between Filipinos and Americans.
(b) To develop true Christian fellowship.
(c) To show the real humanitarian spirit by offering their moral, spiritual, and material aid and protection of the fellow beings; most especially to the fellow members of the federation.
(d) To advance the moral and social conduct of each member.
(e) To foster the educational advancement of each member.
(f) To respect the superiors and office holders of the federation.
(g) To serve in any capacity for the further advancement of the Filipino Federation of America.
(h) To be loyal to the constitution of the federation.
(i) To peacefully obtain the immediate and complete independence of the Philippine Islands.
(j) To work for a fair and truthful understanding of the relations between the United States and the Philippines.
(k) To be an active agency of the solution of the Philippine Islands.

(1) To uphold the Constitution of the United States. To build, construct, erect, purchase, hire, or otherwise acquire or provide any building or office for the purpose of carrying out the objects of the corporation; to solicit memberships in said corporation and the dues or funds derived therefrom, or in any other manner, are to be used in carrying out the objects and purposes for which this corporation is organized. To provide and maintain club rooms for members of the corporation, and to do and perform any and all other matters of things necessary to be done in carrying out the objects and purposes of this corporation.

Third.   That the place where the principal business of said corporation is to be transacted is in the city of Los Angeles, county of Los Angeles, State of California, but this corporation may maintain an office outside of the State of California.

Fourth.   That the term for which said corporation is to exist is 50 years from and after the date of its incorporation.

Fifth.   That the number of directors of said corporation shall be three and the names and residences of the directors who are appointed for the first year and to serve until the election and appointment of their successors are as follows, to wit:

Hilario Camino Moncado, 428 Stack Building, Los Angeles, California.

Andres A. Darilay, 428 Stack Building, Los Angeles, California.

P. R. Alonso, 428 Stack Building, Los Angeles, California.

That on the 30th day of March, 1927, in the county of Los Angeles, in said State of California, an election was held for directors; that all the members of said association were present and voted at such election; and that the result thereof was that the directors hereinbefore named were declared duly elected.

In witness whereof we have set our hands and seal this 31st day of March, A.D. 1927.

Hilario Camino Moncado

Andres A. Darilay

P. R. Alonso

TYDINGS-MCDUFFIE BILL
1934

This is one of the most important laws passed by the Congress of the United States in its relations to the people in the Philippine Islands. Through this law, the Congress created not only the Commonwealth of the Philippine Islands, but also promised its political independence from the United States. This law also restricted the immigration of Filipinos by offering them alien status, although Filipinos were nationals of the United States owing their allegiance to her.

Source: U.S. Congressional Records, Seventy-third Congress, Second Session, 1934, Vol. 78, Part XII, Public No. 127.

To provide for the complete independence of the Philippine Islands, to provide for the adoption of a constitution and a form of government for the Philippine Islands, and for other purposes.

Be it enacted by the Senate and House of Representatives of the United States of America in Congress assembled.

CONVENTION TO FRAME CONSTITUTION
FOR PHILIPPINE ISLANDS

Section 1. The Philippine Legislature is hereby authorized to provide for the election of delegates to a constitutional convention, which shall meet in the hall of the House of Representatives in the capital of the Philippine Islands, at such time as the Philippine Legislature may fix, but not later than October 1, 1934, to formulate and draft a constitution for the government of the Commonwealth of the Philippine Islands, subject to the conditions and qualifications prescribed in this Act, which shall exercise jurisdiction over all the territory ceded to the United States by the treaty of peace concluded between the United States and Spain on the 10th day of December, 1898, the boundaries of which are set forth in Article III of said treaty, together with those islands embraced in the treaty between Spain and the United States concluded at Washington on the 7th day of December, 1900. The Philippine Legislature shall provide for the necessary expenses of such conventions. . . .

Section 8. (a) Effective upon the acceptance of this Act by concurrent resolution of the Philippine Legislature or by a convention called for that purpose, as provided in Section 17.

(1) For the purpose of the Immigration Act of 1917, the Immigration Act of 1924 (except Section 13 (c)), this section and all other laws of the United States relating to the immigration, exclusion, or expulsion of aliens, citizens of the Philippine Islands

who are not citizens of the United States shall be considered as if they were aliens. For such purposes the Philippine Islands shall be considered as a separate country and shall have for each year a quota of fifty. This paragraph shall not apply to a person coming or seeking to come to the Territory of Hawaii who does not apply for and secure an immigration or passport visa, but such immigration shall be determined by the Department of the Interior on the basis of the needs of industries in the Territory of Hawaii. . . .

Section 14. Upon the final and complete withdrawal of American sovereignty over the Philippine Islands the immigration laws of the United States (including all the provisions thereof relating to persons ineligible to citizenship) shall apply to persons who were born in the Philippine Islands to the same extent as in the case of other foreign countries.

CERTAIN STATUTES CONTINUED IN FORCE

Section 15. Except as in this Act otherwise provided, the laws now or hereafter in force in the Philippine Islands shall continue in force in the Commonwealth of the Philippine Islands until altered, amended, or replaced by the Legislature of the Commonwealth of the Philippine Islands or by the Congress of the United States, and all references in such laws to the government or officials of the Philippines of Philippine Islands shall be constructed, insofar as applicable, to refer to the government and corresponding officials respectively of the Philippine Islands. The foremost of the Commonwealth of the Philippine Islands shall be deemed successor to the present government of the Philippine Islands and of all the rights and obligations thereof. Except as otherwise provided in this Act, all laws or parts of laws relating to the present government of the Philippine Islands and its administration are hereby repealed as of the date of the inauguration of the government of the Commonwealth of the Philippine Islands.

Section 16. If any provision of this Act is declared unconstitutional or the applicability thereof to any person or circumstance is held invalid, the validity of the remainder of the Act and the applicability of such provisions to other persons and circumstances shall not be affected thereby.

EFFECTIVE DATE

Section 17. The foregoing provisions of this act shall not take effect until accepted by concurrent resolution of the Philippine Legislature or by a convention called for the purpose of passing upon that question as may be provided by the Philippine Legislature.

PETITION TO PRESIDENT ROOSEVELT
1934

Depression was harsh to Americans, but it was harsher to American minorities. Many Filipinos were not able to find employment, and the unemployed Filipinos were refused public assistance because they were considered alien. Discriminated against by white workers in their effort to find employment, and rejected by public officials in their struggle to receive relief, Filipinos in Salinas, California, decided to send their petition to President Roosevelt.

Source: The Philippines Mail, October 8, 1934.

Honorable Franklin D. Roosevelt
President of the United States of America
Washington, D. C.
Your Excellency:

We, the undersigned natives of the Philippine Islands, residing on the Pacific Coast and engaged in agricultural work, respectfully petition as follows:

Due to the fact that we are Nationals of the United States of America, but not entitled to the rights of full citizenship and not having representation through consular agencies or other duly authorized officials, we find ourselves, in the case of social or economic difficulties, without the facilities of protest or protection afforded to citizens of a foreign country, and though we owe allegiance to the United States government, we have no means through which our rights as a non-citizen group may be protected.

INJURY IMPOSITIONS

We find ourselves accused by the general public of lowering the wage scale by working for lower wages and yet forced by the growers to accept a lower scale than corresponding white labor. With the alternative of being subject to mob violence, the destruction of our homes by fire and to unwarranted arrest, if any action is taken to unite for the purpose of maintaining a higher wage scale.

We find ourselves losing thousands of dollars a year in unpaid wages for employment by citizens of foreign nations, who are well organized and duly represented and who take advantage of the fact that we, as a National group, have no representation.

FILIPINOS DISILLUSIONED

We find ourselves subject to racial prejudice and discrimination in all social relationships, after having been educated in Americanized schools in the Philippine Islands and encouraged to esteem and strive for the civilization typified by Americans.

We have all emigrated to the United States, stimulated by the high ideals of Americanism and desirous of finding a higher and more worthy means of expression, only to be disillusioned on every hand by the experiences of our unsatisfactory social status.

PROTECTION ASKED

We find ourselves, for the most part, forced to live in barns and outbuildings in direct violation of the State housing laws and when we secure camps of the most modern type, having such buildings subject to destruction by incendiary fires, because an attempt is made to demand higher wages through orderly and approved methods.

We therefore ask and beg of you, as President of the United States of America, to take the necessary steps through the proper agencies to set up means by which our interests may be represented and protection to our rights afforded.

REPATRIATION ALTERNATIVE

If this is not possible, we petition you as President of the United States of America, that steps be taken immediately for our repatriation to our native land in the Philippine Islands at government expense, so that we may work out our destiny and future among our own people, where we hope and trust, that even though it may not afford all the seeming advantages of Western Civilization, it may be more conducive to our future happiness.

It is with the greatest esteem and respect for you, our Chief Executive, that we herewith attach our signatures.

FILIPINO REPATRIATION ACT
1935

The seventy-fourth Congress of the United States
passed the House Resolution that became Public
Law No. 202 on July 10, 1935. This law was designed to provide Filipinos returning to the
Philippine Islands with transporation at the government's expense. During the first year of operation, a total of 533 Filipinos were repatriated,
at an average cost of $116 per person. By the end
of the program in December, 1940, a total of 2,190
Filipinos had been sent back to their homeland.

Source: U.S. Congressional Records, Seventy-
fourth Congress, First Session, 1935, Vol. 79,
Part XIV, Public No. 202.

Be it enacted by the Senate and House of Representatives of the United
States of America in Congress assembled. That any native Filipino residing in any State or the District of Columbia on the effective date of this Act,
who desires to return to the Philippine Islands, may apply to the Secretary
of Labor, upon such form as the Secretary may prescribe, through any officer of the Immigration Service for the benefits of this Act. Upon approval
of such application, the Secretary of Labor shall notify wuch Filipino forth-
with, and shall certify to the Secretary of the Navy and the Secretary of War
that such Filipino is eligible to be returned to the Philippine Islands under
the terms of this act. Every Filipino who is so certified shall be entitled
at the expense of the United States, to transportation and maintenance from
his present residence to a port on the west coast of the United States, and
from such port, to passage and maintenance to the port of Manila, Philippine
Islands, on either Navy or Army transports, whenever space on such transports is available, or on any ship of United States registry operated by a
commercial steamship company which has a contract with the Secretary of
Labor as provided in Section 2.

Section 2. The Secretary of Labor is hereby authorized and directed to
enter into contracts with any railroad or other transporation company, for
the transporation from their present residences to a port on the west coast
of the United States of Filipinos eligible under Section 1 to receive such
transportation, and with any commercial steamship company, controlled by
citizens of the United States and operating ships under United States registry,
for transportation and maintenance of such Filipinos from such ports to the
port of Manila, Philippine Islands, at such rates as may be agreed upon between the Secretary and such steamship, railroad, or other transportation
company.

Section 3. The Secretary of Labor is authorized and directed to prescribe such rules and regulations as may be necessary to carry out this
Act, to enter into the necessary arrangements with the Secretary of War
and the Secretary of the Navy to fix the ports on the west coast of the United
States from which any Filipinos shall be transported and the dates upon
which transportation shall be available from such ports, to provide for the
identification of the Filipinos entitled to the benefits of this Act, and to pre-
vent voluntary interruption of the journey between any port on the west coast
of the United States and the port of Manila, Philippine Islands.

Section 4. No Filipino who receives the benefits of this Act shall be entitled to return to the continental United States except as a quota immigrant
under the provisions of Section 8 (a) (1) of the Philippine Independence Act
of March 24, 1934, during the period such of Section 8 (a) (1) is applicable.

Section 5. There is hereby authorized to be appropriated, amounts necessary to carry out the provisions of this Act. All amounts so appropriated shall be administered by the Secretary of Labor, and all expenses, including those incurred by the Navy and War Departments, shall be charged
thereto.

Section 6. No application for the benefits of this Act shall be accepted
by any officer of the Immigration Service after December 1, 1936; and all
benefits under this Act shall finally terminate on December 31, 1936 unless
the journey has been started on or before that date, in which case the journey to Manila shall be completed.

Section 7. Nothing in this Act shall be construed as authority to deport
any native of the Philippine Islands, and no Filipino removed from continental United States under the provisions of the Act shall hereafter be held to
have been deported from the United States.

BRIEF OF ROQUE ESPIRITU DE LA YSLA IN SUPPORT
OF PETITION FOR WRIT OF CERTIORARI
1935

> In this brief Mr. Roque Espiritu De La Ysla ar-
> gues for his just cause in asking for U.S. citizen-
> ship through naturalization. He presents historical
> relations between the inhabitants of the Philippine
> Islands and the government of the United States.

> Source: The Philippines Mail, August 12 and 19,
> 1935.

I.

The opinion of the Circuit Court of Appeals for the Ninth is reported
from pages 29 to 32 inclusive of the Record.

II. -- Jurisdiction

1. The date of judgment to be reviewed is May 20, 1935. (Record 29-
32).

2. The statutory provision which is believed to sustain the jurisdiction of this Court is Judicial Code, Section 240, Subdivision (a); U.S.C.A.
Title 28, Section 347, Subdivision (a).

III. -- Statement

The essential facts are set out in the petition.

IV. -- Specification of Errors

1. There has been such a departure from the real issues of the questions of law involved in the case, or so far sanctioned such departure by
the trial court, as to call for an exercise of this Court's power of supervision, for:

(a) Validity of the Treaty of Peace at Paris, ceding the Philippine
Islands from Spain to the United States, and the Philippines ceased
to be a foreign country;

(b) the Petitioner as a person born subject to the jurisdiction and within the allegiance of the United States--specifically, the 11th day of
April, 1899--by birth, becomes a citizen of the Philippine Islands
and that of the United States; and

(c) Petitioner as a citizen of the Philippines owing permanent allegiance to the United States as a citizen thereof, and not being an
alien, any attempt to naturalize him under the Act of May 9, 1918,
c. 69, 40 Stat. 542; as amended March 2, 1929, c. 536, Sec. 6
(c) (d), 45 Stat. 1514; May 26, 1932, c. 203, Sec. 2 (a) 47 Stat.
163; 8 U.S.C. 339, alleged to be applicable to any native born Filipino, is in violation of the Federal Constitution.

2. The Circuit Court of Appeals has decided a Federal question in a way probably in conflict with the applicable decisions of this Court, for:

(a) The said Court failed to give due weight and consideration of Section 30 of the Naturalization Act of June 29, 1906, c. 3592, 34 Stat. 606; 8 U.S.C. 306; and

(b) The Philippine Islands is an organized territory of the United States and the power of Congress is limited under the Constitution.

3. The Circuit Court of Appeals has decided an important question of general law in a way probably untenable or in conflict with the great weight of authority, for:

(a) There was a total failure to establish the birth right of citizenship as against Petitioner based upon his race, nativity or descent, and the lack of three years' naval service, merely citing Toyota v. United States, 268 U.S. 402, having to do with a Japanese, an alien.

V.--Argument

1. The Circuit Court of Appeals has so far departed from the real issues of the questions of law involved in the case, or so far sanctioned such departure by the trial court, as to call for an exercise of this court's power of supervision, for:

(a) Validity of the Treaty of Peace at Paris, ceding the Philippine Islands from Spain to the United States, definitely transferred the allegiance of the Filipinos from Spain to the United States, and the Philippines ceased to be a foreign country.

The Treaty of Peace with Spain signed at Paris, December 10, 1899, ratified by the United States Senate on February 14, 1899, and proclaimed by the President on April 11, 1899 (30 Stat. 1755, 56 and 69), provided:

Article III.

"Spain cedes to the United States the archipelago known as the Philippine Islands, and comprehending the Islands lying within the following line:
. . .

"The United States will pay to Spain the sum of 20 million dollars ($20,000,000) within three months after the exchange of the ratifications of the present treaty.

Article IX.

"Spanish subjects, natives of the Peninsula, residing in the territory over which Spain by the present treaty relinquishes or cedes her sovereignty, may remain in such territory or may remove therefrom, retaining in either event all their rights of property, including the right to sell or dispose of such property or of its proceeds; and they shall also have the right to carry on their industry, commerce and professions, being subject in respect thereof to such laws as are applicable to other foreigners. In

case they remain in the territory they may preserve their allegiance to the
Crown of Spain by making, before a court of record, within a year from
the date of the exchange of ratification of this treaty, a declaration of their
decision to preserve such allegiance; in default of their decision to preserve such allegiance; in default of which declaration they shall be held to
have renounced it and to have adopted the nationality of the territory in
which they reside.

"The civil rights and political status of the native inhabitants of the territories hereby ceded to the United States shall be determined by the Congress."

There is no dispute as to the validity of the treaty. It is a contract between two Sovereigns, entered into each side, not only in the first instance,
but also by way of ratifications, by persons authorized to bind their respective countries.

It definitely accomplishes one legal result, the Philippine Archipelago
was transferred from Spain to the United States. In the light of international
law, the Islands was acquired by conquest because there was a war followed
by a Treaty of Peace, the right of acquiring sovereign rests upon the Convention, and is therefore founded on contractual cession. The title rested
on the superior strength of the conqueror; this giving the United States a
possession which ripens with lapse of time, or more simply -- as Heim-
burger would say -- assists in the acquisition of "res nullius," (a subject
which is the property of no one).

The Filipinos have thus ceased to owe allegiance and now owe it to the
United States. As regards the status of the native inhabitants of the Philippine Islands, Mr. Hay, then Secretary of State, in circular instructions on
May 2, 1899, to the diplomatic and consular officers of the United States,
declared that, pending legislation by Congress on the subject, they were
entitled to the protection of the United States as against every foreign government; and he directed that when duly registered they should be given
official protection in all matters where a citizen of the United States similarly situated would be entitled thereto. (See Mr. Hay, Secretary of State,
to Mr. Leishman, Minister to Switzerland, December 28, 1900, For. Rel.
1900, page 903).

Mr. Chief Justice Fuller in delivering the opinion of the Court in Fourteen Diamond Rings, Emil J. Pepke, Claimant v. United States, 183 U.S.
176, stated on page 179 the situation of the Philippines under the Treaty as
follows:

"The Philippines thereby ceased, in the language of the
treaty, 'to be Spanish,' (ceasing to be Spanish, they ceased to
be foreign country). They came under the complete and absolute sovereignty and dominion of the United States, and so became territory of the United States over which civil government could be established. The result was the same although
there was no stipulation that the native inhabitants should
be incorporated into the body politic, and none securing to

them the right to choose their nationality. Their allegiance
became due to the United States and they became entitled to
its protection."

In Downes v. Bidwell, 182 U.S. 244, 279, Mr. Justice Brown in an-
nouncing the conclusion and judgment of the Court as to the status of the
inhabitants of the acquired territory, stated:

"We are also of opinion that the power to acquire territory by treaty
implied not only the power to govern such territory, but to prescribe upon
what terms the United States will receive its inhabitants, and their status
shall be in what Chief Justice Marshall termed the 'American Empire.'.
. . that if their inhabitants do not become, immediately upon annexation,
citizens of the United States, their children thereafter born, whether sav-
ages or civilized, are such, and entitled to all the rights, privileges and
immunities of citizens."

Chancellor Kent, in his commentaries, speaking of the general division
of the inhabitants of every country, under the comprehensive title of "Aliens
and Natives," says:

"Natives are all persons born within the jurisdiction and allegiance of
the United States. This is the rule of the common law, without any regard
or reference to the political condition or allegiance of their parents, with
the exception of the children of ambassadors, who are, in theory, born
within the allegiance of the foreign power they represent. . . . (Go Julian
vs. Government of the Philippine Islands 45 Phil. 789, 295).

Again in the concurring opinion of Justice White, Shias and McKenna,
in Downes v. Bidwell, supra, in the course of the opinion in allusion to the
case of the Hawaiian Islands, submit an illustration on page 306;

"Take a case of discovery. Citizens of the United States discover an
unknown island, peopled with an uncivilized race, yet rich in soil, and valu-
able to the United States for commercial and strategic reasons. Clearly,
by the law of nations, the right to ratify such acquisition and thus to acquire, the territory would pertain to the government of the United States."

Speaking as to continuous and useful possession, the Court further proceeded on page 307, stating:

"By the law of nations, recognized by all civilized states, dominion of
new territory may be acquired by discovery and occupation, as well as by
cession or conquest; and when citizens or subjects of one nation, in its
name, and by its authority or with its assent, take and hold actual, continuous and useful possession, (although only for the purpose of carrying on a
particular business, such as catching and curing fish or working mines)
of territory unoccupied by any other government or its citizens, the nation
to which they belong may exercise such jurisdiction and for such period as
it sees fit over territory so acquired."

While passing on this point, may the attention of the Court be directed
to a case having to do with the Philippines, in Kepner v. United States, 195
U.S. 101, 124:

"When Congress came to pass the act of July 1, 1902, it enacted, almost

in the language of the President's instructions, the Bill of Rights of our
Constitution. In view of the expressed declaration of the President, followed
by the action of Congress, both adopting, with little alteration, the provisions
of the Bill of Rights, there would seem to be no room for argument that in
this form it was intended to carry to the Philippine Islands those principles
of our Government which the President declared to be established as rules
of law for the maintenance of Individual freedom, at the same time express-
ing regret that the inhabitants of the islands had not theretofore enjoyed
their benefit."

The Treaty became for the date of its ratification the supreme law of
the land, and the language here is plain and unequivocal.

In the "Treaties, Their Making and Enforcement," Second Edition by
Samuel B. Crandall, in speaking of Effect of Treaty on Status of Territory
and Its Inhabitants, the author said on pages 200-201:

"Upon this change of allegiance, the native inhabitants of the ceded territory are so far impressed with the nationality of the United States as to
be entitled as against all other nations to its protection.

"Under international law the ceded territory: becomes a part of the
nation to which it is annexed; either on the terms stipulated in the treaty
of cession, or on such as its new master shall impose."

Again, Mr. Chief Justice Fuller, in construing the force and effect of
this treaty in the Fourteen Diamond Rings v. United States, supra, stated
on page 178 as follows:

"The Philippines, like Porto Rico, became, by virtue of the treaty,
ceded conquered territory or territory ceded by way of indemnity. . . .

"No reason is perceived for any different ruling as to the Philippines.
By the third article of the treaty Spain ceded to the United States the
archipelago known as the Philippine Islands, and the United States agreed
to pay to Spain the sum of twenty million dollars within three months. The
treaty was ratified; Congress appropriated the money; the ratification was
proclaimed. The treaty-making power; the executive power; the legislative
power, concurred in the completion of the transaction."

On page 180; speaking of the sovereignty and title of Spain over the
Philippines, the distinguished jurist in delivering the opinion of this court
further continued:

"The sovereignty of Spain over the Philippines and possession under
claim of title had existed for a long series of years prior to the war with
the United States. . . . She granted two islands to the United States, and
the grantee in accepting them took nothing less than the whole grant."

If anything further remains to be done or can be done by Congress, or
by any other entity, to more fully vest sovereignty and dominion over the
Philippines in the United States, the method is not apparent.

The role played by the Government in the acquisition of the Philippines,
as all other territory added to our national domain since the Republic was
founded, was simply that of agent and representative of the American people.

In Scott v. Sanford, 60 U.S. (19 Howard 393,448), Mr. Chief Justice Taney discussing this point of agent and representative on the Louisiana Purchase, stated:

"It (Louisiana Territory) was acquired by the General Government as the representative and trustee of the people of the United States, and it must therefore be held in that character for their common and equal benefit; for it was the people of the several states, acting through their agent and representative, the Federal government, who in fact acquired the territory in question, and government holds it for their common use until it shall be associated with the other states as a member of the Union."

(b) The Petitioner as a person born subject to the jurisdiction thereof and within the allegiance of the United States, specifically after the eleventh day of April, 1899, by birth, becomes a citizen of the United States.

Confirming the provisions of the Treaty, supra, Congress by the Act of July 1, 1902, c. 1899, 23 Stat. 632, which provided for the administration of the affairs of civil government in the Philippines, enacted the following Section 4 of the said Act, to wit:

"All inhabitants of the Philippine Islands who were Spanish subjects on the 11th day of April, 1899, and resided in said islands on that date, and their children born subsequent, thereto, shall be deemed and held to be citizens of the Philippine Islands, except such as shall have elected to preserve their allegiance to the Crown of Spain in accordance with the provisions of the treaty of peace between the United States and Spain, signed at Paris, December 10, 1898, and except such others as have since become citizens of some other country: Provided that the Philippine Legislature is authorized to provide by law for the acquisition of Philippine citizenship by those natives of the Philippine Islands who do not come within the foregoing provisions, the natives of the insular possessions of the United States; and such other persons residing in the Philippine Islands who are citizens of the United States or who could become citizens of the United States, under the laws of the United States if residing therein. (August 20, 1916, c. 416, Sec. 2., 39 Stat. 546)."

May Your Petitioner call the attention of the Honorable Court that in the treaty provisions, supra, there exists a change of phraseology with the foregoing Act with respect to inhabitants of the Philippines. The provisions of the treaty in question reads:

"Spanish subjects, natives of the Peninsula, residing in the territory. . . ." and while the Act of July 1, 1902, as amended on August 23, 1918, supra read:

"All inhabitants of the Philippine Islands. . . and their children born subsequent thereto," Congress enlarged the scope as to what was intended by the provisions of the Treaty, supra. In the humble opinion of the Petitioner, the second paragraph of Article IX of the said Treaty, which provided;

"The civil rights and political status of the native inhabitants of the territories hereby ceded to the United States shall be determined by the Congress" is intended to refer to those native inhabitants already residing in the Philippines at the time of the negotiation of the said treaty of peace, and not to any later time.

AN APPEAL TO THE GOVERNMENT OF THE COMMONWEALTH OF THE PHILIPPINE ISLANDS
1937

The members of the Filipino Communities of
America, New Orleans, Louisiana sent the following petition to the government officials of
the Commonwealth of the Philippine Islands asking them to find relief for Filipino seamen who
were faced with the problem of losing their employment as a result of the Merchant Marine
Act of 1936.

Source: The Philippines Mail, October 4, 1937.

WHEREAS, by virtue of the granting of the Commonwealth Government
of the Philippines, the Filipinos residing in the United States became "aliens",
although subjects of the United States till such time when complete relin-
quishment of the United States' sovereignty over the Philippine Islands be
withdrawn; and

WHEREAS, through passage of laws (Washington Statute, Subsidy Act,
Merchant Marine Act of 1936, etc.), the Filipinos in this country have been
deprived of their livelihood especially those who have depended mainly on
Maritime Industry and Federal jobs; and

WHEREAS, as a consequence, the passage of said Merchant Marine
Act, some three to five thousand Filipino seamen who have served aboard
American vessels, majority of whom have over 10 to 15 years of service,
have been driven out of work, with no possibility of future employment; and

WHEREAS, the Filipino non-citizens, who were ejected from the WPA
since the enactment of the Emergency Relief Appropriation Act of 1937, together with their families, are now facing difficulties in their everyday life
which will tend to demoralize their standing in the Community where they
reside; and

WHEREAS, the Filipinos being classified as "aliens" even if they have
families and children born in this country, could hardly secure relief or assistance either from the city or state where they reside, or from the Federal Government of the United States; therefore,

BE IT RESOLVED: That the Filipinos in the United States through the
Filipino Communities of America, New Orleans, Louisiana present an appeal
to the Commonwealth government of the Philippine Islands and its Legislative officials to institute legislation whereby Filipinos in the United States
could be classified as subjects, with the privileges of an American citizen;
and

BE IT FURTHER RESOLVED: That copies of this resolution be sent to
the President, Vice-President and Legislative Officials of the Philippine

Commonwealth Government, Political Leaders, Industrialists, Manufacturers, Businessmen, Labor Union Leaders, Churchmen, and leading newspapers throughout the Islands.

DR. GANCY'S TESTIMONY BEFORE THE 75TH CONGRESS
1938

>Dr. Gancy, president of the Filipino League for
>Social Justice located in New York, gave the follow-
>ing testimony before the Seventy-fifth Congress.
>In his testimony, he defends a testimony given to
>to the same legislative body by a Mr. Emilio Alba
>who represented a group of Brooklyn seamen. Dr.
>Gancy states in his testimony that Filipinos in
>America are as assimilable as any group of immi-
>grants and that discrimination against Filipinos
>is unfair and unjust.

>Source: The Philippines Mail, January 31, 1938.

Gentlemen of the Committee:

On December 3rd, 1937, at the public hearing by this Committee to
amend the Merchant Marine Act of 1936, a Mr. Emilio Alba, representing
a group of Brooklyn seamen, followed me in my testimony here. In the
course of Mr. Alba's testimony some very distasteful points were brought
into the discussion and, therefore, into the record, which should never have
been brought up at all. I refer to the question which Congressman Richard
J. Welch of California injected during the course of his questioning of the
witness: that the Filipinos as a race are unassimilable. The gentleman from
California further said that the Filipinos who are not satisfied with conditions in the United States should avail themselves of the Repatriation Act
and go home, and viciously added: "where you can join your wives and
families, marry into your own race and not with the whites, which is permitted unfortunately in some states of the Union."

IRRELEVANT SUBJECT

The gentleman from California is, of course, entitled as an individual
and as a member of Congress and of this Committee, to voice his own personal stand on the question of Filipino naturalization and immigration, except that this question is not a subject of the hearing as I said before, and
should never have been taken up at all.

Unfortunately for the case of the Filipinos, the witness representing the
Filipino Brooklyn seamen whom Mr. Welch had pummeled mercilessly was
not equal to the task and was evidently not prepared to answer intelligently
and squarely the questions propounded to him by the California solon. The
witness, without a doubt brought the question of "family ties" into the discussion quite innocently and in order only to elucidate the grave economic
and social problems involved in the Filipino seamen's case. This, the gentleman from California took advantage of, and proceeded to inject into the

perfectly innocent statement of a well-meaning, though not any too brilliant
a witness the fact that the presence of Filipinos in this country is most ob-
noxious to many of his constituents and most especially to Congressman
Welch himself.

EXPLAINS ASSIMILATION

Since the gentleman from California has seen fit to inject into the discussion an impertinent phase of the Filipino problem in the United States,
although as I have said before the question has no particular bearing on the
merchant marine revision, and since there has not been an adequate response from the catigated witness, permit me to state briefly to the committee, and particularly to the gentleman from California that naturalization is a formal, legal procedure, giving the alien the right to participate
in the affairs of his adopted country and to receive its protection. I want
to especially impress upon the gentleman from California that naturalization does not mean that the immigrant, or as in the case of Filipinos or
other candidates for naturalization, that they are assimilated as many people seem to think. But it does mean that for some reason or reasons they
are willing to transfer their chief political loyalty.

Assimilation, it must be remembered, is fundamentally a cultural process which implies the acceptance of ideas, attitudes, customs and traditions of a new group. It is rarely, if ever, a completed process, as people
assimilate only on points. On different points, the person isolates, accomo-
dates and assimilates himself.

INVISIBLE AND SUBTLE

A well-known author on Americanization said that "Americanization
is invisible and subtle if it is to be real and enduring. Donning American
clothes and eating American food does not constitute Americanization. It
means divesting one's self of a certain deep-rooted patrimony of ideas,
sentiments, traditions and interests and an acceptance of their participation
in a certain new spiritual inheritance. Such a thing cannot be accomplished
completely in one generation. Even the second generation of European immigrants cannot fully be assimilated."

Filipinos who have come to this country at an early age and who have
lived here for many years are today placed in a situation that presents many
problems for them. They have become Americanized, then disorganized
and then partially at least un-Americanized. As I have already pointed out,
Americanization is a subtle process that many Filipinos do not realize how
completely they have become assimilated until they face certain problems
which sometimes cause disorganization, such as a return to their former
situation. An old American resident of Missouri for instance, did not realize how much of a Missourian he was until he returned to the East Side of
New York. Even Jacob Riis, the celebrated author, had to return to Denmark
to discover that he was an American. Similarly, Filipinos who have been
assimilated have only to reutrn to the Philippines to find out that they are
Americans.

ENEMY OF ASIATICS

The gentleman from California has for years been an enemy of Asiatic labor in his state, especially during the troubled days of 1922 when the question of Chinese and Japanese exclusion from the state was a grave labor issue. I have no quarrel with Mr. Welch on that score. There are some very fine justifications in those cases in favor of Mr. Welch's attitude. Today, however, after he seemingly had cleared the decks of strictly foreign labor problems in his state, he is bent upon the exclusion of the Filipinos and the further imposition of restrictions upon them as a labor as well as a social group. Is Mr. Welch being honest and just about the Filipino problems or is he merely joining public hysteria without due regard to the real political status of the group he especially wishes to castigate?

ACCUSED OF LOWERING WAGES

Filipinos in California and in many parts of the United States are today accused by people who entertain the same viewpoint as the gentleman from California, of working for low wages, of taking jobs from Americans, of living in tenements and shacks and of having a very low standard of living and in few instances were or are accused of saving money to send to their relatives at home.

In considering these questions, we have only to rely more upon logic and reasoning than upon statistical analysis. Statistics, however, show that Filipinos generally receive lower wages than Americans and that wages also vary considerably among the different racial and national groups. It is well also to remember that the general run of Filipinos who come to this country are poor and must work for the wages offered them or starve. They work in most cases for Americans who set the wages they receive; if they peacefully work for the wages offered, they are blamed for their docility; and if they organize and strike for higher wages they are accused of being ruled or led by foreign agitators and radicals.

FALSE ACCUSATION

Equally problematic is the charge that Filipinos take jobs away from Americans. I might say that when Filipinos displace Americans, it seems reasonable to conclude that Americans have secured better positions, that the Filipinos have been more efficient or that Filipino labor has been more profitable to the employer. It is important that Mr. Welch bear in mind that for most parts, Filipinos are engaged in work that Americans refuse to do.

Bad housing conditions are not alone confined to Filipinos, but are frequently found among poor whites of old American stock. Furthermore, Americans own the tenements and shacks which they rent to Filipinos and city fathers permit such buildings to stand and be rented. Their requests for improvement, in many instances, are ignored and if they attempt to move into better neighborhoods, they are generally rudely told that they do not belong there.

FALSE ECONOMIC THEORY

Condemnation of the Filipinos for sending money to the Philippine Islands appears to be based on a false economic theory. A large part of the Filipinos' money goes to pay for their passage to the states or for that of a relative or a friend, or to help their people in the islands. The little money flowing into the Philippines enables the people there to purchase more goods from the United States. This in turn helps American manufacturers and producers to operate more fully and to pay higher wages. Both countries are, therefore, benefited economically. Moreover, the Filipinos give value received for their wages and I see no earthly reason why they should not be free to send it to their needy people at home or do what they please with their money without so much unnecessary condemnation.

Most of the biological arguments against Filipino immigration which the gentleman from California seems to follow, are based on the discredited theory of Nordic superiority. Since there are no pure races and since we have no way of accurately testing inherent racial abilities, this theory if I may so impress upon Mr. Welch, has long been discarded by outstanding authorities on the subject.

UNFAIR TESTS

Psychological tests, in attempts to compare the mental abilities of different racial groups including the Filipinos , have been performed from time to time. Unfortunately, many of the tests and makers of tests found what appears to have existed in their own thinking before the tests were given. They seem to have forgotten that they were endeavoring to test a natural endowment by artificial means and under artificial conditions. As a result they have tested natural attainment rather than innate ability.

Filipino intermarriages with Americans may offer a reasonably secure base from which to begin excursions into the elusive problem of assimilation. Many difficulties are, however, apparent in approaching this question and in employing this method. One is that there are practically no facts on Filipino-American intermarriages in the United States which are available. As to the extent of the fusion, little is known of the rate of which this inter-relationships or race-crossing can be based. It must be pointed out again that whatever work has been done in the problem of assimilation, the same is only observational because of this lack of quantitative data.

INTERMARRIAGE

Permit me also to say to the gentleman from California that while it is true that Asiatics from the barred zone are ineligible for citizenship, yet there are people from Asia, Europe and Africa who are fundamentally Asiatic and Oriental as the people in the barred zone who are perfectly eligible for citizenship.

Probably the prejudices against intermarriages with Filipinos and Americans in this country are not appreciably greater today than the prejudices which have existed in the past by racial groups that intermarry freely now.

As to the assimilibility of Filipinos, and quite contrary to the fixed views of the gentleman from California, let us not lose sight of the fact that they are a perfectly assimilable group. They do not keep their own customs and laws and they are by no means inferior in mental and moral points.

LABOR PROBLEM

It is well also to inform the members of this Committee that the gap in labor supply in California without doubt caused the acceptance of Filipino labor there many years ago. This acceptance immediately preceded the exclusion of Chinese and Japanese labor. Consequently, the Filipinos were welcomed since that time when the State of California was sorely in need of labor to supplant the Chinese and Japanese groups. That was, however, many years ago and since the pressing need for Filipino assistance has passed, they are today similarly treated and highly denounced as a totally unwelcomed group. The treatment and attitude of Mr. Welch and some of his constituents in California was, and is the same attitude they have displayed after the usefulness of the Chinese and Japanese in the development of their vast agricultural lands have ceased. Fortunately, despite the pressure of this perfectly bigoted stand, many Californians are still nice to Filipinos.

I do not, however, condemn altogether the discriminatory and rather vicious attitude of the gentlemen from California, because even the early American colonists after they have developed a sort of national consciousness expressed almost similar apprehension in the influx of foreigners at that time, except that in the present case the subject of Mr. Welch's apprehension are not foreigners but perfectly loyal subjects. As I said, as early as 1751, Benjamin Franklin wrote, "Why should the Palatine boors be suffered to swarm into our settlements and, herding together, establish their language and manners to the exclusion of ours? Why should Pennsylvania, founded by England, become a colony of aliens, who will shortly be so numerous as to Germanize us instead of our Anglifying them?" (Works of Benjamin Franklin, edited by John Bigelaw, Vol. II, p. 233). Some 30 years later, Thomas Jefferson was deploring the fact that foreigners "will infuse into it (U.S. Legislation) their spirit, warp and bias its discretions and render it a heterogenous incoherent distracted mass?" (The Writings of Thomas Jefferson, edited by Paul L. Ford, Vol. II, p. 190).

CONFLICTING THEORIES

In brief, the whole attitude of the people of the United States toward immigration has been one of conflicting practices and theories. So long as they had a sparsely settled country and a scarcity of labor, many Americans were generously hospitable. As a consequence the United States has become a haven for the poor and the oppressed of other lands.

We have seen two divergent and quite impracticable laws on immigration control: unrestricted immigration and absolute exclusion. Between these extremes is the per centum limitation, which is devoid of logic. It represents a fear psychosis, lest the country admit too many. But it does not take into consideration how many can be assimilated, the special type of economic development needed, or the personal worth of the individual. At best, it gives a method for reducing numbers, the base of which may be shifted at any time. On the whole, I might say that Americans accept the theory of Nordic superiority; that they believe Protestants are likely to make better citizens than persons of other religious views; that an illiterate man is capable of becoming a good citizen, and that only inferior representatives of racial groups desire to emigrate.

In conclusion, gentlemen of the Committee, cordial reception, attempted assimilation, brusque restrictions and hysterical exclusion--these four phases tell the story of many Californians toward the Filipino. Congressman Welch only restated it here.

VARONA APPEALS FOR UNITY
1939

Mr. Francisco Varona, head of the Nations Division of the Philippine Resident Commissioner's Office, Washington, D.C., sent the following letter to the Board of Officers of the Filipino Agricultural Laborers' Association in order to encourage Filipino laborers to unite for the common cause of raising the standard of living by receiving a higher wage than was presently paid to the Filipino laborers.

Source: The Philippines Mail, May 13, 1939.

May 3, 1939

To the Filipino Laborers of San Joaquin and Sacramento Valleys,
Through the Board of Officers of the Filipino Agricultural Laborers'
    Association
    Greetings:
    I appeal to all the Filipino laborers of San Joaquin and Sacramento Valleys to make good their solemn pledge to our Flag to keep the Filipino Agricultrual Laborers' Association alive and strong.
    This Association has been the powerful and only weapon with which they won the strike last month. That victory can never be repeated anymore, if you let your unity die through indifference and neglect. So that the Association may lead a vigourous life, every one should pay his dues as soon as possible. Your contributions will make possible the realization of your cherished dream--to have a Hall of your own within whose walls further negotiations with the Growers for a Uniform Contract and for the solution of your others claims would be made and put into effect by your own elected officers. This Hall should serve as the monument by which the growers and laborers alike, as well as the American public, will remember with respect the now historical date, April 7, 1939.
    I have, and Resident Commissioner Elizalde as well, the utmost confidence in your elected officials, namely President Dr. Macario D. Bautista, Vice-President Lamberto Malinab, your active Secretary, your trusted Treasurer and your courageous delegates from Sacramento, Elias Cabradilla and Ted C. Market.
    Remember our struggle for betterment has just started; it is not yet finished.
    And remember, further, that in Unity alone lies our victory.
    Disorganized, we will fail, and lose all we have gained heretofore, including the respect of our employers.

Hoping to see you all again some time in July, One and United,
Yours for a solid and strong Filipino Agricultural Laborers' Association,
(Signed)   FRANCISCO VARONA.

PROGRAM FOR FILIPINO AGRICULTURAL LABORERS'
ASSOCIATION
1939

Dr. Macario D. Baustista, president of the Filipino
Agricultural Laborers' Association, delivered the
following message in order to present to the members of the Filipino Agricultural Laborers' Association its program for the construction of a Filipino community center.

Source: The Philippines Mail, May 13, 1939.

The Filipino Agricultural Laborers' Association, the organization which
Honorable Varona formed, is now functioning, and Filipino workers, even
those in other agricultural pursuits not related to asparagus, are rallying
under its banner, happy in the thought that at last, they are united under the
guidance of their own government.

Our Association is planning many projects, and the first of these is our
First Annual Convention. This is to take place in Stockton on June 25 this
year. We shall have business meetings during the day, and at night we shall
hold our Grand Inaugural Ball. The city of Stockton, through the convention
bureau, is letting us use the whole Civic Memorial Auditorium FREE for
this convention. We are trying to have Honorable Varona as our guest of
honor at this convention.

Our next big project, in fact our biggest, is the building of our headquarters. This building was stressed by Honorable Varona as vitally needed
by all Filipinos in the territory and by the organization. It will be a building our people can justly be proud of. It will be a monument to the unity of
the Filipinos in this section of the United States, a unity inspired and fos-
tered by the President of our country through the office of our Resident Commissioner and Honorable Varona.

This building will serve as our Community Center. It shall be, first of
all, a recreational center where our people may gather together and play
wholesome games, read newspapers and magazines from the Philippines
and from here. It will have a big meeting hall on the second floor, offices,
stores on the first floor, and possibly a big gymnasium in the basement, de-
pending on the amount of money we shall have.

Students of the social problems of our people, as well as intelligent laymen, have long conceded that the solution to these problems lies in not fighting to eliminate the degrading influences in their social life, but in finding
a substitute for them. This building and recreational center will be our
substitute, and when this shall have been erected, our people should be thank-
ful to our government officials, to our fellow countrymen from Sacramento,
and Stockton, who are working unceasingly for this project, and to the mem-

bers of the Filipino Agricultural Laborers' Association whose money is
going to make this wonderful thing come true.

This unity of our people which will make possible the creation of this
building has already inspired us to engage in other big undertakings. Big
business ventures have been discussed. . . .

As honorable Varona had repeatedly told us in mass meetings and in private conversations, it is up to us to help ourselves first before our government helps us. We started to help ourselves when we held our successful
convention in Sacramento last year. All the things that have come to pass
since then which have finally culminated in the formation of our Association
are results of that memorable convention.

Now our government would like to see that we continue helping ourselves.
Our country would like to see that we keep up this Association which Honorable Varona formed for us. We have her guidance at all times as well as
her moral and material assistance, and our task is not a hard one.

Let us show our beloved President, His Excellency, Manuel L. Quezon,
that we know how to help ourselves, and that we know how to cooperate with
our government. Our President is vitally interested in our well-being here.
During our asparagus trouble he was constantly in touch with our Resident
Commissioner in Washington. His interest in us was shown last year when
he sent Honorable Varona here to inquire into our social and economic conditions. As a result of that investigation, the Philippine Resident Commissioner's Office created its Nationals Division which is headed by Honorable
Varona. This Division is only for Filipinos in the United States and its territories outside the Philippines. The Filipino Agricultural Laborers' Association is responsible to this Division, and periodically sends reports of
everything it does or contemplates doing to that office.

After we have erected our building in Stockton, we shall strive to build
one in Sacramento, for that city is another center of Filipinos. The members of the Association in the Sacramento district are many, and they are
contributing their money for the erection of our building in Stockton. We
have agreed to build the Stockton building first because this is the recommendation and wish of Honorable Varona.

It is the belief held by many that this Association is for the asparagus
workers only. This is not true. This Association is for all Filipino workers,
all Filipino toilers. Our Constitution says: "The membership of this Association shall be composed of all Filipinos working in the agricultural and
allied industries and those engaged in other pursuits, regardless of sex, re-
ligions, or political beliefs or affiliations.

Join the Association now so that we can work together, hand in hand, with
the guidance of our government, to pursue a program for our betterment.

AN APPEAL FOR U.S. CITIZENSHIP
1940

Mr. Trinidad A. Rojo, a graduate of the University of Washington and sociologist who has
written on the subject of Filipino immigrants
in the United States, points out unfair, unjust,
and irrational aspects of the government policy that has continuously denied Filipinos the
right to become U.S. citizens through naturalization.

Source: The Philippines Mail, February 26, 1940.

DUTIES AND RIGHTS MUST CORRESPOND

For your information and entertainment, let me point out to you the
melodramatic inconsistancies of the international law governing Filipino-
American relation on naturalization rights. We, Filipinos, owe allegiance
to the United States. In case of war we are duty bound to lay down our lives
for the STARS AND STRIPES. If the American flag imposes upon us the
duty to die for it, if necessary; in all fairness, it must also give us the
right to live as American citizens if we choose to do so. If the American
flag does not do this, it crucifies the ideals of justice and democracy for
which it stands. Bear in mind, that when a flag loses its symbolism, it is
nothing more than a piece of colorful and embroidered cloth.

BIOLOGICALLY INCONSISTENT

Why are we denied naturalization rights? Is it because we, brown people,
are darker than the whites? That we are darker than the whites is an undis-
putable biological fact. But it is also an irrefutable fact that we are not
darker than the original Americans. The Indians, who by the way, according to anthropology, were Asiaticis, who came to this country 10,000 years
ago when Alaska and Siberia were still connected with a land bridge. It is
also an incontrovertible fact that we are lighter than the African Negroes
who are eligible for American citizenship.

ILLOGICAL

Why are we denied naturalization rights? Is it because we once fought
against America when it forced its sovereignty over us? But there were Ger-
mans who fought against America under the Kaiser in 1917-1918 who later
migrated to American and became U.S. citizens. There will be Nazi subjects of Hitler who will migrate to America in the future and will apply and

be accepted as American citizens. Yet, we who, if any emergency arises, if war breaks between American and Germany, can be drafted to fight against Hitler are not eligible for citizenship. In fact, some of our people joined the war against the Kaiser. Under what principle of ethics and justice, human or divine, can you justify this legal discrimination against us?

UNINTELLIGENT

Why are we denied eligibility for U.S. citizenship? Is it because we are illiterate? There are Filipinos studying in the Colleges and Universities of America, such as the University of Washington, Stanford, Chicago, Harvard, Columbia, Yale, Cornell, etc. Some of them have acquired bachelor, master and doctor's degrees. They are not eligible for citizenship. There are naturalized citizens of this country from Europe who have not even passed the grammar school. There are 300 Filipinos working in the post office of Chicago and there are over a hundred Filipinos holding Federal jobs as clerks in Government Offices in Washington, D.C. They are not eligible for citizenship. There are Filipino veteran labor leaders who have worked and fought with American labor leaders for social and economic justice. They are not eligible for citizenship. There, however, are exceptions to the law. Filipinos who served in the Navy and Army for two or three years and who were discharged honorably are eligible for citizenship. Does this mean that a Filipino sailor makes a better American citizen than a Filipino professor, or a Filipino labor leader, like Vicente O. Naven, who by the way, is also a college graduate? If so, better tear down the STATUE OF LIBERTY and put in its place the STATUE OF MARS, the GOD OF MILITARISM, the GOD OF WAR.

ANALOGOUS

We are denied eligibility for U.S. citizenship. Are you afraid we will crowd you out of your jobs and out of your lands? But whether we want it or not we are here already. Moreover there are only 45,000 Filipinos in the entire continental United States. Due to the fact that their sex ratio is one female to fourteen males, few of them will be left in the next generation. How can 45,000 seize your country? They can not even seize the City of Aberdeen.

As it has been stated, the Indians, former Asiatics, were the original owners of this country. When the Europeans came to this continent, they did not take the trouble of applying for naturalization rights to the Indians. We understand, they simply declared themselves the new bosses of the land; and the Indians left by bullets and bayonets were told to preserve themselves in a museum of living species, called INDIAN RESERVATIONS. Our situation is different. We came here because Americans went to the Philippines. In the first two decades of American occupation of the Islands, American statesmen pursued a policy of "benevolent assimilation." In 1902 the American government sent one thousand American teachers to propagate American culture in the Philippines. They urged Filipinos to come and study here. The American movies and press presented to us an America that is glamourous, romantic and fabulously rich. All in all we were given the impression that America is the land of unlimited opportunities, where every family has a car, and everyone is free and equal.

Contractors in the Alaskan canneries sometimes went to the Philippines and recruited workers there. The Hawaiian sugar and pineapple plantations established recruiting agencies in the thickly populated provinces in the Philippines. The shipping companies, such as the Dollar Line and Canadian Line aid its provincial agents $5.00 for every passenger they could get for America. I may say that America invited itself with the gun to the Philippines, and that we were not only invited, but were also bribed to come to America.

We came to America, in the main, youthful immigrants to drink at the fountain of learning, to see that STATUE OF LIBERTY, to share in the plentitude of the land of millionaires and multi-millionaires. In many cases our rosy dreams were shattered to pieces on the rocks of realities. We notice that the world message of the STATUE OF LIBERTY is annihilated by racial prejudices and that the wheels of the Chariot of Mammon crushes economic opportunity. As long as we accepted low wages and intolerable conditions, the exploiters professed to love us even more than their fellow countrymen --white workers. But when we begin to learn real Americanism, when we organized ourselves into unions, and when, finally we affiliated with American organized labor, the exploiters became sick of indigestion due to sour grapes; for now they profess not to like us.

You see, we are victims of Philippine-American relationship which started before most of us Filipinos now in America were born. Certainly we are not responsible for that relationship. In fact, our forefathers opposed it in a war which lasted over three years. Now we are here because America is in the Philippines. We are asking you no special privilege. We simply ask you to grant us the naturalization rights which the Americans in the Philippines enjoy in our government.

From the standpoint of biology, color line, history, anthropology, logic, justice, fairness, and world's democracy, your naturalization law is consistently inconsistent toward us. It is a record against you rather than against us. But we do not blame you American people, for our case has never been presented to you. The metropolitan press usually misrepresents us to the public. But now that I have presented our case to you, I am sure that you want to rectify the law governing our relationship, and that you will stand by the Statue of Liberty whose world message is "SHARE WITH US THE BLESSINGS OF FREEDOM, JUSTICE, AND DEMOCRACY, IRRESPECTIVE OF CREED, COLOR, RACE OR NATIONALITY."

A DECLARATION OF POLICY
1940

Mr. Macardo G. Collado, president of the
Filipino Community of Salinas, California,
delivered the following speech that set forth
his administration's policy for the people of
the Filipino Community of Salinas during his
tenure.

Source: The Philippines Mail, April 30, 1940.

Ladies and Gentlemen:
      We are privileged at this time to meet together for the purpose of dis-
cussing among ourselves the best policy of our administration which we
think would be compatible with the dignity and honor of our people in our
Community. Since its formation, our Community has marched on progres-
sively because of the patriotic cooperation of our leaders who have always
been unselfish in responding to the needs of our people.
      I have been privileged for the second time to be at the head of our Com-
munity administration and today I am deeply concerned like you all are with
a consistency in our administration that will promote the best interests and
welfare of our people in this valley and in the vicinity. I deem that the success of our administration lies in our ability to comprehend the problems
of our people and after comprehending them, to offer solutions from time
to time. I deem also that any man at the head of an administration can be
successful only with a proper teamwork accorded him by his colleagues.
I therefore deem it advisable and proper to consult with you in order to get
the benefit of your advice before imparting to our people the general policy
of our administration. For the good of our Community, this administration
shall pursue a policy of mutual consultation among the elective and appoin-
tive officials. That I am convinced, will be conducive to progress.
      In view of all this, I have the honor to offer to you for your advice and
recommendation the following as basic policies of our administration:

Departmental Functions
      Finance. -- The Department of Finance shall conduct legitimate cam-
paigns for the purpose of raising funds for our Community. There are Community expenditures that may be too burdensome for our people if collected
by process of regular taxation. There are charity expenditures that come
up from time to time; they deserve our most whole-hearted attention. There
are civic expenditures that cannot be ignored because they are consistent
with the progress of our Community. All these and many more must be
taken into consideration with reference to intelligent financing.
      Business and Economics. -- This department shall study the progress

of our Community in legitimate business. There have been several instances
of this progress especially in merchandising among our people in the valley.
Patronage of Filipino business must be encouraged with greater emphasis.
Preference to local business among our people must also be encouraged.
Traveling merchants, promoters and peddlers from other localities must
be made to conform with Community practices so as to insure better and
more profitable cooperation.

Athletics and Recreation. -- This department shall promote the physi-
cal upbuilding of our people in the valley. It shall have the direct management of our athletic activities among our people. It shall hold programs
featuring sports and athletic competition from time to time. It shall study
the possibility of holding athletic programs with other Communities so as
to promote sports and athletics fellowship with our people in other localities.

Labor. -- This department shall cooperate with legitimate labor organizations and government agencies so as to safeguard the welfare of our laborers in the valley. The time probably has not yet come for our Community to take the initiative in labor organizing but if that time should come, it
must be at the behest of the greater number of our bona fide resident laborers. We believe in the maintenance of the present status quo in the valley until public welfare demands any change--if at all.

The Community recognizes the leadership of the National Division of
the Philippine Resident Commissioner's office in Washington, D.C. and will
submit all its recommendations to the National Division.

Education and Spiritual Welfare. -- This department will attempt to
promote popular education among our colonists in things Philippine. There
is in our Community a growing second generation which should be acquain-
ted with the fine culture and tradition and ideals of our country; there is a
great preponderance of our colonists whose spiritual welfare should be en-
hanced not only through the media of ecclesiastical services but also through
laymen's services.

The spiritual leadership of our administration in this Community shall
not be dogmatic but fluid. It shall recognize no sector denominations of any
kind; it shall provide spiritual comfort to our people in cooperation with
any Church organization provided such organization does not promote any
particular denomination as against another denomination.

Health and Sanitation. -- This department shall look after the health
of our Community. It shall cooperate with government agencies in the promotion of better health among our colonists. It shall help our people in ob-
serving the laws that promote sanitation.

Social Welfare. -- This department shall promote the social welfare
of our people. It shall help in providing our people with clean and wholesome social outlet among them. It shall seek to substitute a condition of
social stagnation with a condition of social progress. It shall cooperate with
social welfare agencies with view to promoting Community welfare.

Publicity and Propaganda. -- This department shall study ways and
means of wholesome publicity in behalf of the Community. It shall at all

times seek to discriminate the wholesome from the unwholesome methods of Community publicity; it shall attempt to conduct a propaganda system which will redound to the honor and good name of the term "Filipino." It shall always be alert in counteracting any system of false publicity against our people.

It shall always seek to promote and protect the good name of our Community through printed matters.

Public Relations. -- This department shall promote the welfare of the Community in good neighborly relations with other races. It shall help improve our people's interracial relations with other nationalities; it shall help improve Philippine-American relations which is most essential to our progress in this country.

These are brief sketches of our departmental functions. Each head of the department in cooperation with his members shall function as a separate agency of our Community and each department is given a free hand in expanding its activities according to the demands of the time and the progress of our Community. Each department shall enjoy the right of presiding over executive meetings as long as such meetings pertain to any particular departmental activities. The President of the Community shall act as ex officio chairman of such meetings. To promote cooperation among departments, other departments are urged to attend such meetings as may be called by any particular department. This is consistent with our basic policy of mutual consultation among administrative officials.

In this manner cooperation and fellowship among department heads and members shall be harmoniously promoted and regular teamwork shall bind all officials to a common undertaking.

Organic Constitution

Our Community has progressed to an extent that requires an organic constitution as a foundation of its government. It recommends to your consideration the drafting of our Community Constitution. I ask your permission to allow me to appoint a committee for such purpose; I also ask you to submit your recommendations for consideration of said committee.

Reports to the National Division

All activities of our Community shall be recorded and reported to the National Division of the Philippine Resident Commissioner's office in Washington. Departmental activities shall be properly reported, duly signed by the heads of the departments and attested to by the proper executive officials.

TO ALL FILIPINOS IN THE UNITED STATES, ITS
TERRITORIES AND POSSESSIONS (EXCLUDING THE PHILIPPINES)
1940

> Mr. J.M. Elizalde, Resident Commissioner of
> the Philippines to the United States, sent the fol-
> lowing message to all Filipinos in the United
> States to obey the law by registering, as required
> of all alien Filipinos in the United States and its
> territories under the Alien Registration Act of
> 1940.

Source: The Philippines Mail, September 16, 1940.

The Attorney General of the United States has rendered the opinion that for the purposes of the Alien Registration Act of 1940, Filipinos are to be classified as "aliens." As a consequence, the registration will be required of all Filipinos residing in the United States (this term comprises the States, the Territories of Alaska and Hawaii, the District of Columbia, Puerto Rico, and the Virgin Islands) who have not acquired United States citizenship.

The most important provisions of the Alien Registration Act can be condensed as follows:

1. No visa shall be issued to any alien seeking to enter the United States unless said alien has been registered and fingerprinted in the Consulate issuing the visa.

2. It shall be the duty of every alien now or hereafter in the United States, who is fourteen (14) years of age or older, to register and be fingerprinted; with respect to persons less than 14 years of age, it shall be the duty of their parents or legal guardians to apply for their registration;

3. The provisions of the law referring to registration and fingerprinting will take effect sixty (60) days after its enactment (the law was approved on June 28, 1940);

4. All applications for registration and fingerprinting shall be made at post offices or such other places as may be designated by the Commissioner of Immigration and Naturalization;

5. Failure to register and be fingerprinted carries a maximum penalty of $1,000 or a six-month imprisonment, or both, and;

6. Changes of address should be made known in writing within five days after such a change to the Commissioner of Immigration and Naturalization; failure to do so carries a penalty of $100 fine or a 30-day imprisonment, or both.

Although I most respectfully disagree with the Attorney General in an opinion that places us in the same category as persons owing allegiance to a foreign power, disregarding our oath of allegiance to the United States, I urge under the circumstances that all Filipinos cooperate whole-heartedly

with the Federal authorities in achieving the objectives of the Alien Registration Act.

The registration of all those persons who are not citizens of the United
States (even in the case of those who have obtained their second papers) has
been required by law not only as a means of identification, but to protect
their interests during these difficult times. In this connection I deem it op-
portune to quote the Honorable Francis Biddle, Solicitor General of the
United States, on the subject:

"We are requiring registration of foreigners not only as a means of identification, but to protect their interests during these difficult times. . . .

"Registration records will, in accordance with the provisions of the Act,
be secret and confidential, and will be available only to persons designated
by the Commissioner, with the approval of the Attorney General, so that
NO ONE MAY HAVE ANY FEAR THAT THESE RECORDS WILL BE USED
BY EMPLOYERS OR LABOR FOR BLACKLISTS OR FOR THE PURPOSE OF
DISCRIMINATING AGAINST ALIENS.

"Since the principal object of the law is to enable us to have an accurate
identification of every non-citizen, the law also requires that all who register shall be fingerprinted. Now, I realize that this may sound unpleasant
to some people, but it is not meant to be so. I was fingerprinted as was
everyone else who joined the Army and Navy during the Great War: and
thousands of decent citizens are voluntarily fingerprinted today by the Federal Bureau of Investigation." When he signed the Act, the President of the
United States said:

"The alien registration act of 1940. . . . should be interpreted and administered as a program designed not only for the protection of the country
but also for the protection of the loyal aliens who are its guests. The registration. . . .does not carry with it any stigma or implication of hostility
towards those who, while they may not be citizens, are loyal to this country
and its institutions. Most of the aliens in this country are people who came
here because they believed and had faith in the principles of American democracy, and they are entitled to an must receive full protection of the law.
IT WOULD BE UNFORTUNATE IF, IN THE COURSE OF THIS REGULATIVE
PROGRAM, ANY LOYAL ALIENS WERE SUBJECT TO HARASSMENT."

Concerning the fear expressed to me by some of our citizens that the net
of registration and fingerprinting may operate in some cases to prejudice
them in their employment, I discussed this phase of the problem with the
Secretary of the Interior and I am pleased to advise that under date of August 17, 1940, the Honorable Harold L. Ickes wrote to me as follows: "I am
well aware of the fact this requirement may affect the interests of Filipino
citizens in private employment but I assure you that this Department will
be glad to cooperate in any way to protect the interests of Filipino employees
who may be adversely affected.

If you will bring to my attention any cases which may arise whereby Filipino citizens are unjustly discriminated against by reason of this law, I will
be very happy to do everything possible to secure relief."

Lastly, I suggest that when Filipinos register, they should fill the blank corresponding to the required statement of their nationality with the following notation:

"Citizen of the Philippines, owing allegiance to the United States."

August 26, 1940.

(Signed)   J.M. ELIZALDE,
                                      Resident Commissioner of the
                                      Philippines to the United States.

MESSAGE OF COMMISIONER ELIZALDE TO THE
FILIPINOS IN THE UNITED STATES
1941

Mr. J.M. Elizalde, Resident Commissioner of
the Philippines to Washington, D.C., issued a
statement on December 8, 1941, urging Filipinos
to cooperate with proper authorities for the protection of the United States.

Source: The Philippines Mail, December 22, 1941.

The crucial hour, which we all had feverently hoped could be averted, is
at hand. The United States and our country are now at war with Japan.

The Philippines is rapidly becoming a vast battleground. Bombs have
been dropped in many places where once resided a peaceful and home-lov-
ing people.

We have faith in the courage and strength of our families and countrymen
to make the severest sacrifices which may be demanded of them. We, who
are here and are comparatively safe from danger, must be prepared to
share the hardships and sufferings of our people which an unprovoked war
has brought and will bring to them.

We must cooperate with the authorities in our communities in all that
they do for the protection of the United States and the cause for which she
stands. Offer your services to the Civilian Defense Councils; present your-
selves to the authorities and give any help that you may be able to render.
Above all, be ready at all times to show that you are a true Filipino and a
loyal national of the United States.

The Office of the Resident Commissioner of the Philippines to the United
States is ready to assist you in any way whatsoever, and furnish you with
unmistakable evidence of your Philippine nationality in the form of a Certificate of Identity.

Plans are under way to enable Filipinos to enlist in the armed forces of
the United States. When the time comes, let us all defend the land we love
and the United States, which has so steadfastly guided and protected us to
this very moment, the most critical in our history.

Washington, D.C., December 8, 1941

J.M. Elizalde

A RESOLUTION ON THE FORMATION OF
FILIPINO ARMY UNITS
1942

The following letter was written by Mr. Juan B. Sarmiento, editor of The Philippines Mail and chairman of the Committee on Resolution of the Formation of Filipino Army Units, to Mr. Henry L. Stimson, secretary of war. Enclosed with the letter was a full text of the resolution.

Source: The Philippines Mail, February 17, 1942.

Honorable Henry L. Stimson
Secretary of War
Washington, D. C.
Dear Sir:

"I respectfully transmit herewith a copy of a resolution on the formation of Filipino army units.

"The resolution expresses the sentiments on this subject of an overwhelming majority of Filipino residents in continental United States.

"Should the War Department act favorably in this matter, the Filipinos, I am sure, will consider it as a further expression of Uncle Sam's friendship to them.

Very respectfully yours,
(Signed)   Juan B. Sarmiento, Chairman,
                Committee on Resolution on the
                Formation of Filipino Army
                Units''

Full text of the Resolution:

"A Resolution On The Formation Of Filipino Army Units

"Whereas, Public Law 360–77th Congress approved by the President on December 20, 1941, makes it possible for Filipinos to serve in the United States Army.

"Whereas, a great number of Filipinos will want to volunteer for induction with the armed forces of the United States.

"Whereas, it is believed that those who would do so could serve more effectively if they were organized into unit or units of their own, under American and Filipino officers, and

"Whereas, after undergoing the necessary training the Filipino unit or units should be, if practicable, sent to the Philippines for duties there, therefore

"Be it resolved, by the Committee appointed at a mass meeting of Filipinos in San Francisco, California, on January 5, 1942, to draft this resolution, that it recommends to the War Department of the United States the formation of Filipino army unit or units, the personnel of which is to be made up of Filipinos who volunteer for induction or are drafted into the armed forces of the United States.

"Be it further resolved, that the following be each furnished a copy of this resolution:

"His Excellency, Franklin Delano Roosevelt, President of the United States,

"His Excellency, Manuel L. Quezon, President of the Philippines,

"Honorable Henry L. Stimson, Secretary of War,

"Honorable Joaquin M. Elizdale, Resident Commissioner of the Philippines to the United States.

"Resolution Committee:

Juan B. Sarmiento, Chairman-President, Filipino Community of Solano County, Editor, The Philippines Mail.

Juan M. Dulay, President, Filipino Community of San Francisco, Inc.

Pacita Todtod, President, Filipino Community of San Jose.

Celestino T. Alfafara, Vice-Grand Master, C.D.A., Inc.

OF SECOND GENERATION FILIPINOS
1944

This speech was delivered to the participants of the Sixth Filipino Inter-Community Conference held in Fresno, California,
on September 11-14, 1944. The speaker, Miss Carmen Padilla,
urges the first generation Filipinos to teach their sons and
daughters about their native land, its people, and their culture.

Source: The Philippines Mail, September 28, 1944.

Mr. Chairman, Ladies and Gentlemen of the Convention:

It is with some temerity that I stand before you this afternoon to
deliver this short address. For you not only represent the cream of
Filipino leadership on the Pacific Coast; you are also the elders of our
various communities. I, who represent the second generation--the
groping, inarticulate second generation--have found the courage to defy
that time-honored parental injunction, "Children should be seen and
not heard," only because I believe that the time has come when our
parents should give us the opportunity to realize our potentialities so
that we may contribute what we can, no matter how inadequate or how
meager, to the rebuilding of our devastated land. For although we have
never seen our country, our hearts bleed for her, almost as much as
yours do. Our sorrows are as poignant as yours, our anger towards the
invader as violent, our determination to help rebuild our motherland as
inflexible.

These are the days of youth. Throughout this war-torn world,
wherever an outraged humanity fights for decency and noble ideals,
on every field of battle, the flower of youth is sacrificed in order that
the glorious heritage of freemen might live and grow, and be enjoyed
by all people. In the hallowed grounds of Bataan, thousands upon thousands of our youth willingly gave their lives so that we and the genera-
tions to come might enjoy that very freedom for which they fought and
died.

We of the second generation also know the anguish and the agony
of war, the bitterness of separation from our loved ones, the pain that
heroes suffer before they die. We of the second generation have grown
old before our time. We now know, just as you know, sorrow and suffering.

But we have no complaints. We have no regrets that we will not
enjoy our youth with careless abandon as you enjoyed yours when peace
was upon this earth and goodwill reigned over the world. For this holo-
caust was thrust upon us by evil men. It is not of our choosing that war
is upon us. We who have tasted freedom know that we must earn freedom
by fighting for it. Freedom, as Colonel Carlos P. Romulo, the last man
off Bataan, has truly said, is not handed down to us on a silver platter.

We are earning that freedom. And because our cause is righteous, we know we will have freedom. Because we are in the right, we will achieve victory! Of that we are sure.

On the other side of the world across a stretch of ocean, eight thousand miles away, a freedom-loving country lies wrapped in silence. She is your country. She is our country. She is the Philippines. She awaits American and Filipino youth from these shores to free her from her heavy chain of bondage. She yearns for peace--she hopes that when freedom comes, her people will be prosperous and happy.

The youth of any nation is truly its greatest national asset. If that youth is given the proper training, the proper guidance, and the proper understanding that it deserves, it will develop into a generation fully capable of assuming the tremendous responsibilities of the postwar era.

We of the second generation appeal to you, our elders, to guide us, to help us discover the best that is within ourselves so that those of us who will come back from the battlefields, those of us who are left behind, contribute not only towards the securing and maintenance of permanent world peace, but also towards the prosperity of our country and, the happiness of our people. We of the second generation are inarticulate. We have not voiced, up to now, our desires to participate in your planning for a better Filipino community; for a better Filipino nation in America, and of more importance, for a still greater and stronger nation in the Philippines. We want you to know that we want to participate in that planning.

But to do so, we must know more about our country. Insofar as the Philippines is concerned, we of the second generation are groping in the darkness of ignorance. What we know of our country we learned through hearsay or through speeches delivered during Rizal Days. There has been little, if any, systematic attempt on the part of our elders to enlighten us. There has been little, if any, effort to stir in us a deep feeling of national pride in the achievements of our people, in the richness of their cultural heritage, in the burning passion which is rooted in their hearts to rise as a nation worthy of the respect and admiration of freemen everywhere. Our elders have failed to chart a course for us to follow so we might orient our thinking, orient our ambitions towards the development of a great Philippines!

We do not mean to say that you have been remiss in the obligation--civilized man has come to consider this an obligation--to educate your children. On the contrary, Filipino parents have been used and are obsessed with the desire to give their children here the education which they were not fortunate enough to have. But they have not collectively planned to educate us as to the needs of our country so that we may learn to acquire these particular skills necessary to develop her resources.

Other immigrants to this country, as soon as they were settled down sufficiently to have families and children, did not forget that these children needed to be taught certain fundamental and necessary things concerning the land of their parents' birth. They built schools for them; they organized community centers where both the old and the young can gather together to listen to folktales, to see folk dances, to hear the story of the building of their nation. . . .

In this way, they hoped to give their children the opportunity to view life from the perspective of a great materialistic civilization and their own unhurried, idealistic one. In this way, they hoped to mold the minds and character of their children into a pattern which they considered best for them. This is what other immigrants--for example, the Chinese--have accomplished for their children.

Are not we deserving of similar beneficial attention? Why cannot our elders accomplish this too? Are there valid arguments that they should not? Are not we to be given a chance to draw from both civilizations the best things that are in them with which to enrich our lives and the lives of our children? Are not we to be given a chance to prepare ourselves to take some part in the development of our country-- the country which for all practical purposes, is foreign to us?

This is the question which we of the second generation ask of you. This is what we ask of our government. Help us find ourselves, guide us so that we may be able to use our best capabilities in the difficult task of nation rebuilding. Remove that veil of darkness which covers our eyes so that we may see the road ahead--the road towards prosperity and abundance for our motherland. Show us how best we can use our training, our education, our skills, and technical knowledge when this task of rebuilding comes. Our contribution towards that end may appear small but we will gladly give it, and we want it to be the best we can give. For we are a part of the Filipino nation, and we are indeed proud of it.

PROBLEM OF UNDEREMPLOYMENT OF FILIPINOS
1969

The following is an article written by George Pena, a contributing editor for the Philippines Mail. The author points out a
major problem that faces a large number of Filipino immigrants, particularly those who are highly educated in their
country, but whose education is not recognized by various agencies in America that are responsible for certifying people before they are judged qualified to engage in their respective profession.

Source: The Philippines Mail, July 1969.

In the old days which only real old-timer Filipinos can recall
with bitterness and frustration specially among those who had had
adequate educational background, the problem of underemployment was
there but the early immigrant Filipinos which came in hundreds to
the United States from 1924 to 1935 (the beginning of the Philippine
Commonwealth) were mostly concerned in securing a living so that
even though at home they had never dirtied their fingers at least many
of them were forced by economic reasons to accept menial types of
labors like working in farms, picking fruits, picking tomatoes, cutting
asparagus and harvesting lettuce. So generally speaking, seventy percent of the early Filipino immigrants were farm workers, apartment
and hotel janitors, dishwashers, etc. Those who were not able to endure
the outdoor field work became school boys for survival, houseboys,
family cooks, chauffeurs and as butlers if they had learned the technique
of serving a'la family style.
        The educated, those with college education as well as those with
degree in their pocket were the real underemployed, for they had no
place to use their talent or college degrees. Being deprived of applying
for U.S. citizenship for the immigration laws forbid the naturalization
of orientals and non-whites for U.S. citizenship, they were unable to
compete in civil service examinations, to work for government agencies.
Because of rampant discrimination, they were not able to secure
clerical employment with private industries. Not even employment
agencies where service for fee was charged, accepted Filipinos to
register for employment.
        Because of inability of the American public and institutions dis-
pensing above menial jobs to understand the need of giving employment
to Filipinos who considered themselves underemployed, the hundreds
of educated Filipinos continued to work as janitors, cooks, butlers,
waiters and chauffeurs. Many became foremen in farms and there-by
assumed a little supervisory position among our countrymen. The only
real prestige for non-citizen Filipinos was the post-office job as

laborers. These post office Filipino workers were paid by the Federal
government but were not under civil services rules and regulations.

The under-employed Filipinos--those who got bachelor or master
degrees returned to the Philippines. Those who didn't find utopia in
going home stayed and stayed as menial workers like the educated
Chinese, Japanese and Negros who were as badly discriminated in
securing the right job in order to be properly employed in positions
most suitable to education.

The end of the second world war improved the outlook of the
old-timers. Many returned to college, to special technical schools,
leased farm lands to become producers of farm products, others got
jobs above the menial type of works as lowly clericals, sales works
in department store, hamburger cooks, insurance agents, and apartment owners. The old timers who had college education competed in
civil service jobs and took clerical jobs. Even though many have bach-
elors and even master degrees, they were and are still unable to get
beyond the clerical positions for promotional examinations or higher
job classification required experience qualification which the educated
Filipinos lack for after all their experiences prior to Pearl Harbor
and as far back as 1956 were mostly menials and therefore unable to
qualify for higher job. And even if they were able to pass the oral interview usually was their downfall for they are given failing grade.

The Negro movement for equality of opportunity regardless of race
ignited the forward surge of minorities in securing better than menial
and clerical jobs. Because of Negro demonstrations against discrimination in job opportunity, housing, school integration and other set
backs the Black man and Black woman suffered for nearly two-hundred
years, the public as well as private sectors of the population began to
realize that the minorities need better of everything that the white man
enjoys. Negros, Chinese and Japanese because of the militancy and
vigorous pursuit of what is good for the whites is also good for them,
began occuring more responsible positions in private and government
agencies. The Filipinos not being organized and meekly vocal, continue
to pursue the attitude of getting a job not in line or in tune with educational training.

Three waves of Filipino immigration came to the United States.
The first one started in 1920 to 1935. Those early immigrant Filipinos
were mostly laborers with springlings of high school graduates and
few with college educational background. They became the menial
workers for no skill jobs were opened for them as they were ineligibled
for U.S. citizenship and besides discrimination against non-whites was
religiously practiced both by the public and private industries.

The second wave started during the end of world war II. Filipinos
who were affluent student sons and daughters of the wealthy Filipinos,
visitors bulging with dollars, and exchange visitors visa holder came
in hundreds. The second wave stayed temporarily in the country. They
were not permitted by law to work, nor stay permanently. But somehow
many found employment by other means like by marrying American
citizens and thereby becoming permanent residents or by simply asking
for permit to work due to financial hardships. Others just worked and
challenged the officials to find them.

The third wave started after the liberalization of the immigration law by allowing 20,000 immigrants to enter the states annually from one country. This law resulted in the avalanche flow of Filipinos to the United States the last four years. This time the American embassy in Manila processed much faster the visas of applicant teachers, doctors, nurses, engineers, accountants, dentists, pharmacists and degreed Filipinos to enter the United States for permanent residence.

The flow of professional Filipinos to the United States created the problem of underemployment to these degreed college educated English speaking Filipinos. Because of the lack of experience of both governmental and private industries to know the efficiency and capabilities of the newly arrived Filipino professionals, they became underemployed. It simply means they are in the wrong jobs doing clerical, sales work, janitorial and menial works when they are supposed to be teaching if they are teachers or as engineers doing engineering skills.

Unless the Filipino organizations in the United States, specially in California where there is a large concentrating of university educated and technically skilled Filipinos, unite together and like the Negros demand better job opportunities for the educated Filipinos, like the Filipino Old Timers who were menial workers for nearly three decades, the newly arrived Filipino professionals who are now parts and parcels of this great United States will continue to be job discriminated unless the 75,000 Filipinos in California and some 200,000 in the fifty states become more vocal and militant like the Negros who want to correct the injustices of being underemployed.

The idea of being satisfied, being employed even though underemployment can project a bad image for all Filipino professionals. It is for this very reason that all articulate Filipinos must do something to correct this false image that is being built in the employment of Filipino teachers, engineers, doctors, accountants and all degreed just arrived Filipinos to the United States as clerks and menial workers.

When we become underemployed we become second class U.S. citizens. This situation must not continue to exist forever.

BIBLIOGRAPHY

BIBLIOGRAPHY OF SELECTED REFERENCES

I.   General Bibliographies

Alcantara, Reuben R. The Filipinos in Hawaii: An Annotated Biblio-
    graphy. Honolulu: Social Science Research Institute, University
    of Hawaii, 1972.

II.   Books and Monographs

Bogardus, Emory Stephen. Anti-Filipino Race Riots: A Report Made
    to The Ingram Institute of Social Science of San Diego. San Diego:
    T. G. Dawson for Ingram Inst., 1930.

_____. "Filipino Americans." One America. Ed. Francis J. Brown
    and J. S. Roucek. New York: Prentice-Hall, 1945, pp. 354-63.

_____. "Filipino Americans." Our Racial and National Minorities.
    Ed. Francis J. Brown and Joseph S. Roucek. New York: Prentice-
    Hall, 1939, pp. 510-25.

_____. Immigration and Race Attitudes. New York: Health, 1928.

Bottomley, A. W. T. A Statement Concerning the Sugar Industry in
    Hawaii; Labor Conditions on Hawaiian Sugar Plantations; Filipino
    Laborers Thereon, and the Alleged Filipino "Strike" of 1924,
    Honolulu: Honolulu Advertiser Pr., 1924.

Buaken, Manuel. I Have Lived with the American People. Caldwell,
    Idaho: Caxton Printers, 1948.

. "No Orientals are Wanted Here." Race Prejudice and Dis-
    crimination: Readings in Intergroup Relations in the United States.
    Ed. Arnold Rose. New York: Knopf, 1951, pp. 270-6.

Bulosan, Carlos. America Is in the Heart, a Personal History. New
    York: Harcourt, Brace, 1946.

_____. Chorus for America: Six Philippine Poets. Ed. Carlos
    Bulosan. Fwd. Dion O'Donnol. Los Angeles: Wagon and Star
    Pub., 1942.

_____. Letter from America. Prairie City, Ill.: Pr. of James A.
    Decker, 1942.

_____. Sound of Falling Light; Letters in Exile. Ed. Dolores S.
    Feria. Quezon City: n.p., 1960.

Burma, John H. Spanish-Speaking Groups in the United States. Durham, N. C.: Duke Univ. Pr., 1954, pp. 138-55.

Cariaga, Roman R. The Filipinos in Hawaii; Economic and Social Conditions, 1906-1936. Honolulu: Filipino Public Relations Bur., 1937.

Cressey, Paul G. The Taxi-Dance Hall. Chicago: Univ. of Chicago Pr., 1932.

Cruz, Hermenegildo. "Problems of Filipino Emigration." Problems of the Pacific, 1931: Proceedings of the Fourth Conference, Hangchow and Shanghai, China, Oct. 21 to Nov. 2, 1931. Institute of Pacific Relations. Chicago: Univ. of Chicago Pr., 1932, pp. 431-7, pp. 460-61.

Feria, Benny F. Filipino Son. Boston: Meador Pub., 1954.

Hooper, H. Elston. "A Filipino in California Copes with Anxiety." Clinical Studies in Culture Conflict. Ed. Georgene H. Seward. New York: Ronald Pr., 1958, pp. 265-90.

Kirk, Grayson. "The Filipinos." Race Prejudice and Discrimination: Readings in Intergroup Relations in the United States. Ed. Arnold Rose. New York: Knopf, 1951, pp. 38-42.

Konvitz, Milton Ridvas. The Alien and the Asiatic in American Law. Ithaca: Cornell Univ. Pr., 1946.

Lasker, Bruno. Filipino Immigration to Continental United States and to Hawaii. Pub. for American Council, Institute of Pacific Relations. Chicago: Univ. of Chicago Pr., 1931. (Rpt. New York: Arno Pr., 1969).

Manlapit, Pablo. Filipinos Fight for Justice; Case of the Filipino Laborers in the Big Strike of 1924, Territory of Hawaii. Honolulu: Kumalae Pub., 1933.

Manzon, Maximo C. The Strange Case of the Filipinos in the United States. New York: American Committee for the Protection of the Foreign Born, 1938.

McWilliams, Carey. Brothers under the Skin. Boston: Little, Brown, 1943, pp. 176-201, 224-54.

————. Factories in the Field: The Story of the Migrant Farm Labor in California. Boston: Little, Brown, 1940.

Miller, Carey Dunlap et al. Foods Used by Filipinos in Hawaii. Honolulu: Univ. of Hawaii Agricultural Experiment Station, 1946.

Munoz, Alfredo N. The Filipinos in America. Los Angeles: Mountain-
view Publishers, 1971.

Nicanor, Precioso M. Profiles of Notable Filipinos in the U. S. A.,
Vol. I. Intr. Melquiades Gamboa. Fwd. Mauro Baradi. New York:
Pre-Mer Pub., 1963.

Respicio, F. A., ed. Hawaii's Filipinos and Their Part in the War; a
Pictorial Record of Their Work for Victory and Freedom. Honolulu: F. A. Respicio, 1945.

Saniel, J. M. The Filipino Exclusion Movement, 1927-1935. Quezon
City, Philippines, 1967.

Wentworth, Edna Louise. Filipino Plantation Workers in Hawaii: a
Study of Incomes, Expenditures and Living Standards of Filipino
Families on an Hawaiian Sugar Plantation. San Francisco, etc.:
American Council, Inst. of Pacific Relations, 1941.

_____. Living Standards of Filipino Families on an Hawaiian Sugar
Plantation. Honolulu: Hawaii Group, American Council, Inst. of
Pacific Relations, 1936.

                    III.   Periodical Articles

Adeva, Manuel A. "Filipino Students in the United States." Mid-Pacific
Mag., 44 (Aug. 1932), 119-23.

"Alaska--a Filipino Refuge." Mid-Pacific Mag., 42 (Nov. 1931), 437-9.

Alcantara, Reuben R. "The Filipino Wedding in Waialua, Hawaii: Ritual
Retention and Ethnic Subculture in a New Setting." Amerasia.
Vol. 1, no. 4, February 1972, 1-12.

Anthony, Donald Elliot. "Filipino Labor in Central California." Social
and Soc. Res., 16 (Nov.-Dec. 1931), 149-56.

Ballard, Walter J. "Filipino Students in the United States." Jour. of
Education (Boston), 67 (Mar. 5, 1908), 272.

Bierman, Jessie M. and French, Fern E. "Ecological Influences on
Infant Mortality among Japanese and Filipino Immigrants to
Hawaii." Jour. of Tropical Pediat. and African Child Health 9
(June 1963), 3-13.

Bogardus, Emory S. "American Attitudes toward Filipinos." Sociol.
and Soc. Res., 14 (Sept.-Oct. 1929), 59-69.

_____. "Citizenship for Filipinos." Sociol. and Soc. Res., 29 (Sept.-
Oct. 1944), 51-4.

_____. "Filipino Immigrant Attitudes." Sociol. and Soc. Res., 14 (May-June 1930), 469-79.

_____. "The Filipino Immigrant Problem." Sociol. and Soc. Res., 13 (May-June 1929), 472-9.

_____. "The Filipino Immigration Situation." Pan-Pacific Progress, 12 (Jan. 1930), 17-19.

_____. "The Filipino Press in the United States." Sociol. and Soc. Res., 18 (July-Aug. 1934), 581-5.

_____. "Filipino Repatriation." Sociol. and Soc. Res., 21 (Sept.-Oct. 1936), 67-71.

_____. "Foreign Migrations Within United States Territory: The Situation of the Filipino People." Proc. of the National Conf. of Soc. Work, 56 (1929), 573-9.

_____. "What Race Are Filipinos?" Sociol. and Soc. Res., 16 (Jan.-Feb. 1932), 274-9.

Bowler, Alida C. "Social Hygiene in Racial Problems: the Filipino." Jour. of Soc. Hygiene, 18 (Nov. 1932), 452-6.

Buaken, Iris Brown. "My Brave New World." Asia, 43 (May 1943), 268-70.

_____. "You Can't Marry a Filipino; Not If You Live in California." Commonweal, 41 (Mar. 16, 1945), 534-7.

Buaken, Manuel. "Our Fighting Love for Freedom: 1200 Members of First Filipino Infantry Take Oath of Allegiance Which Makes Them Citizens." Asia, 43 (June 1943), 347-9.

_____. "Where Is the Heart of America?" New Republic, 103 (Sept. 23, 1940), 410.

Bulosan, Carlos. "As Long As the Grass Shall Grow." Common Ground, 9 (Summer 1949), 38-43.

Bundy, T. W. "Needs of the Filipinos." Missionary Rev. of the World, 57 (June 1934), 289.

Burma, John H. "The Background of the Current Situation for Filipino-Americans." Soc. Forces, 30 (Oct. 1951), 42-8.

_____. "Interethnic Marriage in Los Angeles, 1948-1959." Soc. Forces, 42 (Dec. 1963), 156-65.

Cariaga, Roman R. "Filipino Fliers Train for Service." Pan-Pacific, 1 (Jan.-Mar. 1937), 53.

_____. "Filipinos in Hawaii." Pan-Pacific, 2 (Jan.-Mar. 1938), 72-3.

_____. "The Filipinos in Honolulu." Soc. Science, 10 (Jan. 1935), 39-46.

_____. "Kapuripuri. A Word Concerning the Contribution of the Filipinos in Hawaii." Mid-Pacific Mag., 49 (Jan.-Mar. 1936), 34-8.

Carreon, Manual L. "Educational Research and Statistics: Measuring the Achievement and Ability of Filipinos." School and Society, 17 (May 5, 1923), 502-4.

Catapusan, Benicio T. "Filipino Immigrants and Public Relief in the United States." Sociol. and Soc. Res., 23 (July-Aug. 1939), 546-54.

_____. "Filipino Intermarriage Problems in the United States." Sociol. and Soc. Res., 22 (Jan.-Feb. 1938), 265-72.

_____. "The Filipino Labor Cycle in the United States." Sociol. and Soc. Res., 19 (Sept.-Oct. 1934), 61-3.

_____. "Filipino Repatriates in the Philippines." Sociol. and Soc. Res. 21 (Sept.-Oct. 1936), 72-7.

_____. "The Filipinos and the Labor Unions." Amer. Federationist, 47 (Feb. 1940), 173-6.

_____. "Leisure Time Problems of Filipino Immigrants." Sociol. and Soc. Res., 24 (July-Aug. 1940), 541-9.

_____. "Problems of Filipino Students in America." Sociol. and Soc. Res., 26 (Nov.-Dec. 1941), 146-53.

"Causes of California's Race Riots." Literary Digest, 104 (Feb. 15, 1930), 12.

Corpus, Severino F. "Second Generation Filipinos in Los Angeles." Sociol. and Soc. Res., 22 (May-June 1938) 446-51.

Deseo, Jose G. "The Filipinos in America." Missionary Rev. of the World, 57 (June 1934), 288-9.

de Vera, Pedro C. "Restrictions of Filipino Immigration to the United States." Pan-Pacific Progress, 14 (Jan. 1931), 38-9.

Feria, R. T. "War and Status of Filipino Immigrants." Sociology and Social Research. 31 (September-October 1946), 48-53.

Kalayaan Editorial Collective. "Filipinos: A Fast Growing U. S. Minority--Philippines Revolution." In Roots, ed. by A. Tachiki, pp. 312-15. Los Angeles: Continental Graphics, 1971.

Keely, Charles B. "Philippine Migration: Internal Movements and Emigration to the United States." International Migration Review, Vol. 7, No. 22, Summer 1973. 177-187.

Kirk, Grayson. "The Filipinos." Annals of the Amer. Acad. of Pol. and Soc. Science, 223 (Sept. 1942), 45-8.

Kolarz, Walter. "The Melting-Pot in the Pacific." The Listener, 52 (Oct. 28, 1954), 702-4.

Konvitz, Milton R. "The Constitution and the Filipinos--Exclusion and Naturalization." Common Ground, 6 (Winter 1946), 101-3.

Lasker, Bruno. "Filipinos in California." Amerasia, 3 (Feb. 1940), 575-9.

_____. "In the Alaska Fish Canneries." Mid-Pacific Mag., 43 (Apr. 1932) 335-8.

_____. "The Philippine Model." Far Eastern Survey, 11 (Nov. 30, 1942), 240-1.

Ligot, Cayetano. "The Filipinos in the Territory of Hawaii." Mid-Pacific Mag. 49 (Jan.-Mar. 1936), 27.

McWilliams, Carey. "Exit the Filipino." Nation, 141 (Sept. 4, 1935), 265.

_____. "Thirty-Six Thousand New Aliens in California." Pacific Weekly, 5 (Aug. 24, 1936), 119-21.

Melendy, H. Brett. "California's Discrimination Against Filipinos, 1927-1935." In Racism in California, ed. by R. Daniels and S. C. Olin, Jr., 141-151. New York: Macmillan, 1972.

_____. "Filipinos in the United States." Pacific Historical Review, Vol. XLIII, No. 4, November 1974, 520-547.

Missemer, George W. "Why the Californians Mob the Filipinos." China Weekly, 51 (Feb. 8, 1930), 353.

"Naturalization of Filipinos." Far Eastern Survey, 14 (Jan. 17, 1945) 9-10.

Nystrom, Gertrude Hill. "America As Filipino Students See It." Religious Education, 28 (Feb. 1933), 149-54.

_____. "The Measurement of Filipino Attitudes toward America by Use of the Thurstone Technique." Jour. of Soc. Psychol. 4 (May 1933), 249-52.

Redadtrini, Ildefonzo. "University of Washington Filipino Alumni." Mid-Pacific Mag. 49 (Jan.-Mar. 1936), 25-6.

"Reflections: the Filipino Immigrant to Hawaii, Exclude the Filipinos, a Filipino's View." Pacific Affairs, 3 (April 1930), 399-401. (Editorial comment on three newspaper articles.)

Rojo, Trinidad A. "A Message to Filipino Undergraduates." Mid-Pacific Mag. 42 (Mar. 1932), 371-3.

_____. "Social Maladjustment among Filipinos in the United States." Sociol. and Soc. Res., 21 (May-June 1937), 447-57.

Santos, Alfonso P. "A Filipino Race in the Making." Sociol. and Soc. Res. 24 (Nov.-Dec. 1939), 158-62.

Santos, Bienvenido N. "Filipinos in War." Far Eastern Survey, 11 (Nov. 30, 1942), 249-50.

Santos, Francisco O. "Metabolism Experiments with Filipino Students in the United States." Philippine Jour. of Science, 23 (July 1923), 51-66.

Sargent, Aaron M. "Survey of Filipino Immigration--Report of Immigration Section." Commonwealth (San Francisco), 5 (Nov. 5, 1929), 312-20.

Scharrenberg, Paul. "Filipinos Demand Special Privileges." Amer. Federationist, 46 (Dec. 1939), 1350-53.

Schibsby, Marian. "Immigration from the Philippino Islands." Foreign Lang. Information Service Interpreter Release, 11 (Aug. 10, 1934), 169-71.

"They Also Serve Filipinos." Newsweek, 76 (Nov. 9, 1970), 32-3.

Villanueva, N. C. "Filipino Business Evolution in Hawaii." Pan-Pacific, 2 (Jan.-Mar. 1938), 63-4.

Vite, Doroteo V. "A Filipino Rookie in Uncle Sam's Army." Asia, 42 (Oct. 1942), 564-6.

Whitney, Philip B. "Forgotten Minority-Filipinos in the United States." In Bulletin of Bibliography. Vol. 29, no. 3, July-Sept. 1972, 73-83.

Wingo, James G. "The First Filipino Regiment." Asia, 42 (Oct. 1942), 562-3.

IV. Documents, including periodical articles

California Dept. of Industrial Relations. Facts about Filipino Immigration into California. Louis Bloch, Statistician. San Francisco: Calif. State Printing Office, 1930, 76p. (Special Bull. no. 3).

California, State Fair Employment Practices Commission. Californians of Japanese, Chinese, and Filipino Ancestry: Population, Education, Employment Income. San Francisco: Calif. State F.E.P.C., Divn. of Industrial Relations, 1965, 52p.

Duff, Donald F. and Arthur, Ransom J. "Between Two Worlds: Filipinos in the United States Navy." Amer. Jour. of Psychiat., 123 (Jan. 1967), 836-43.

"Emigration of the Filipino Laborers Abroad." Labor: Bull. of the (Philippines) Bur. of Labor, 8:27 (1929), 104-7.

Feria, R. T. "War and the Status of Filipino Immigrants." Sociol. and Soc. Res., 31 (Sept.-Oct. 1946), 48-53.

"Filipino Contract Laborers in Hawaii." Monthly Labor Rev., 23 (Oct. 1926), 684-9.

"Filipino in California." U. S. Bur. of Labor Statistics Bull., 541 (Sept. 1931), 290-91.

"Filipino Labor in Hawaii." International Labor Rev., 15 (Apr. 1927), 581-6.

"Filipino Problem in California." Monthly Labor Rev., 30 (June 1930), 1270-75.

"Filipino Baiting in California Has Started." Nation, 161 (July 28, 1945), 71.

"Filipino Fashions." Paradise of the Pacific, 60 (Feb. 1948), 10-11.

"Filipino Immigration." Trans. of the Commonwealth Club. (San Francisco: 24:7 (1929), 307-78.

"The Filipino Question at the Honolulu Pan-Pacific Club." Mid-Pacific Mag., 32 (Nov. 1926), 449-58.

"The Filipinos Do Not Understand." Asia, 43 (Sept. 1943), 560.

Finney, Joseph C. "Psychiatry and Multiculturality in Hawaii." International Jour. of Soc. Psychiat., 9 (Winter 1963), 5-11.

Foster, Nellie. "The Legal Status of Filipino Intermarriages in California." Sociol. and Soc. Res., 16 (May-June 1932), 441-54.

Goethe, C. M. "Filipino Immigration Viewed As a Peril." Current History, 34 (June 1931), 353-4.

Gonzalo, D. F. "Social Adjustments of Filipinos in America." Sociol. and Soc. Res., 14 (Nov.-Dec. 1929), 166-73.

Gorospe, Otilio R. "Making Filipino History in Hawaii." Mid-Pacific Mag., 45 (Mar. 1933), 241-53.

Hurrey, Charles D. "Filipino Students." Inst. of International Education News Bull., 8 (Feb. 1933), 12-13.

"In June--Honolulu's Fiesta Filipina." Sunset, 124 (June 1960), 50.

Inselberg, Rachel Marzan. "Causation and Manifestations of Emotional Behavior in Filipino Children." Child Devel. 29 (June 1958), 249-54.

Jenks, Albert Ernest. "Assimilation in the Philippines as Interpreted in Terms of Assimilation in America." Amer. Jour. of Sociol. 19 (May 1914), 773-91.

Labarthe, Darwin R. et al. "Coronary Risk Factors of Male Workers on a Kauai, Hawaii Plantation: Comparison of Data for Japanese and Filipinos." Public Health Repts. 85 (Nov. 1970), 975-80.

"Migration of Philippine Labor to Hawaii, 1928 to 1932." Monthly Labor Rev., 38 (May 1934), 1267-8.

_____, 1929-1933." Monthly Labor Rev., 40 (May 1935), 1416.

_____. 1932-1936." Monthly Labor Rev., 45 (Sept. 1937), 613.

Moncado, Hilario Camino. Filipino Labor Conditions in the Territory of Hawaii. Report by Hon. Dr. Hilario C. Moncado, Senior Delegate to the Philippines Constitutional Convention to Hon. Manuel L. Quezon, President of the Philippines. Honolulu: n.p. 1936, 39p.

Pendleton, E. C. "Characteristics of the Labor Force." Monthly Labor Rev., 78 (Dec. 1955), 1416-21.

Philippine Commission. Report of the Superintendent of Filipino Students in the United States Covering the Filipino Student Movement from Its Inception to June 30, 1904. Washington: U. S. War Dept., Bur. of Insular Affairs, Philippine Commission, 1905, pt. 3, pp. 919-30.

Philippine Islands. Resident Labor Commissioner's Office, Honolulu, T. H. Authoritative Statement Relative to Filipino Laborers in Hawaii. Report of Hon. Cavetano Ligot, Resident Labor Commission.

Prince, Eleanor G. Naturalization of Certain Specially Exempted Classes, Including Filipinos, Veterans and Seamen. Washington: U. S. Immig. and Naturalization Serv., 1934, 10p. (Immig. and Naturalization Serv. Lectures, 2nd series, no. 29).

"Recent Migration of Filipino Labor to Continental United States and Hawaii." Monthly Labor Rev., 35 (Oct. 1932), 988.

"Report of the Director of Labor to His Excellency the Governor General of the Philippine Islands." Labor: Bull. of the (Philippines) Bur. of Labor, 7:25 (Mar. 1926), 64p.

U. S. Bureau of Insular Affairs. "Filipino Emigration to the United States and Hawaii." U. S. Bureau of Insular Affairs Report(s) to the Secretary of War, 1932-1935.

_____. "Filipino Students in the United States," U. S. Bureau of Insular Affairs Report(s) to the Secretary of War, 1904-1911, 1913-1914.

U. S. Congress. House of Representatives. Admission of Filipinos to the Naval Academy. To Accompany H. R. 6698. House Rept. 2258, 80th C., 2nd s., 1948, 2p. (Ser. 11212).

_____. Agreement on Amendments to a Bill Relating to the Right of Filipinos and East Indians to Become Naturalized Citizens of the United States and to Enter the Country under Small Quotas. To Accompany H. R. 3517. House Rept. 2334, 79th C., 2nd s., 1946, 1p. (Ser. 11025).

_____. Authorizing the Naturalization of Filipinos. To Accompany H. R. 4826. House Rept. 1940, 78th C., 2nd s., 1944, 6p. (Ser. 10848).

_____. Same. To Accompany H. R. 776. House Rept. 252, 79th C., 1st s., 1945, 4p. (Ser. 10931).

_____. Emigration of Filipinos from the United States. To Accompany H. R. 6464. House Rept. 622, 74th C., 1st s., 1935, 5p. (Ser. 9887).

_____. Filipinos in the Naval Reserve. To Accompany H. J. R. 90. House Rept. 143, 80th C., 1st s., 1947, 3p. (Ser. 11118).

_____. Permitting Filipinos to Become Members of the Coast Guard Reserve. To Accompany H. R. 7455. House Rept. 2491, 77th C., 2nd s., 1942, 4p. (Ser. 10664).

_____. Provide for Transportation to the Philippine Islands of Indigent Filipinos Resident in the United States and Territories. To Accompany H. J. R. 71. House Rept. 74, 74th C., 1st s., 1935, 7p. (Ser. 9886).

_____, Providing Means by Which Certain Filipinos Can Emigrate from the United States. To Accompany H. R. 4646. House Rept. 198, 76th C., 1st s., 1939, 2p. (Ser. 10297).

_____. Return of Certain Filipinos to Philippine Islands. To Accompany H. J. R. 118. House Rept. 127, 73rd C., 1st s., 1933, 6p. (Ser. 9774).

_____, To Extend the Period for Emigration of Filipinos from the United States to the Philippine Islands. To Accompany H. R. 9991. House Rept. 2004, 74th C., 2nd s., 1936, 3p. (Ser. 9992).

_____. To Further Extend the Period for Emigration of Filipinos from the United States to the Philippine Islands. To Accompany H. R. 2305. House Rept. 216, 75th C., 1st s., 1937, 3p. (Ser. 10083).

_____. Committee on Armed Service. Hearings on H. R. 6698, Authorizing the Course of Instruction at the United States Naval Academy to Be Given to Not Exceeding Four Persons at a Time from the Republic of the Philippines. Hearing 270, 80th C., 1948, v. 5, pp. 6787-88.

_____. Subcommittee Hearing on H. J. R. 90 to Correct an Error in the Act Approved Aug. 10, 1946 (Pub. Law 720, 79th Congress, 2nd Session) Relating to the Composition of the Naval Reserve. Hearing 73, 80th C., 1947, v. 1, pp. 993-6.

_____, Committee on Immigration and Naturalization. Hearings on Exclusion of Immigration from the Philippine Islands, H. R. 8708. 71st C., 2nd s., 1930, v. 1, 300p.

_____, Naturalization of Filipinos: Hearings Nov. 22, 1944 on H. R. 2012, 2776, 3633, 4003, 4229 and 4826. 78th C., 2nd s., 1944, 59p.

_____. Return to Philippine Islands Unemployed Filipinos. Hearings 72.2.1, H. J. R. 549, 577. 72nd C., 2nd s., 1933, 51p.

_____. Amending the Coast Guard Auxiliary and Reserve Act of 1941. As Amended, So As to Enable Filipinos to Qualify for Service Thereunder. To Accompany H. R. 7455. Senate Rept. 1636, 77th C., 2nd s., 1942, 4p. (Ser. 10659).

_____. Authorizing the Course of Instruction at the United States Naval Academy to Be Given to Not Exceeding Four Persons at a Time from the Republic of the Philippines. To Accompany H. R. 6698. Senate Rept. 1766, 80th C., 2nd s., 1948, 3p. (Ser. 11208).

_____. Authorizing the Naturalization of Filipinos. To Accompany H. R. 776. Senate Rept. 1439, 79th C., 2nd s., 1946, 3p. (Ser. 11016).

_____. Emigration of Filipinos from the United States. To Accompany H. R. 6464, Senate Rept. 849, 74th C., 1st s., 1935, 2p. (Ser. 9879).

_____. Extend the Period for Emigration of Filipinos from the United States to the Philippine Islands. To Accompany H. R. 9991 (S. 3729). Senate Rept. 2031, 74th C., 2nd s., 1936, 3p. (Ser. 9989).

_____. Facilitating the Entry of Philippine Traders. Senate Rept. 1464, 83rd C., 2nd s., 1954, 4p. (Ser. 11729).

_____. Filipinos in Naval Reserve. To Accompany H. J. R. 90. Senate Rept. 136, 80th C., 1st s., 1947, 2p. (Ser. 11114).

_____. Further Extend the Period for Emigration of Filipinos from the United States to the Philippine Islands. To Accompany H. R. 2305. Senate Rept. 427, 75th C., 1st s., 1937, 3p. (Ser. 10076).

_____. Providing Means by Which Certain Filipinos Can Emigrate from the United States. To Accompany H. R. 4646. Senate Rept. 756, 76th C., 1st s., 1939, 2p. (Ser. 10294).

_____. Transporting Filipinos to the Philippine Islands, 1937-- Dec. 31, 1938. Senate Doc. 106, 76th C., 1st s., 1939, 3p. (Ser. 10316).

U. S. Divn. of Territories and Island Possessions. Filipino Immigration to Hawaii, 1901-1946. Washington: National Archives, Record Grp. 126, 1953. 1 reel microfilm.

V.   Newspapers and Periodicals

Ang Abyan, V.1-? Honolulu: Hawaiian Evangelical Assn., 1916-32?.

Bagumbayan. No. 1. New York: Filipino Students Christian Movement in America, 1928.

Caballero. A Philippine News Magazine. V.1, nos. 1-2?. San Francisco: Caballeros de Dimas-Alang, 1952?.

Commonwealth Courier. V.1-? Seattle: R. V. Santos Pub. Co., etc., 1931?-?.

Commonwealth Times. V.1? Santa Maria, Calif., Los Angeles: Filipino Workers in California, 1936?-?.

Filamerican. V. 1-10. Honolulu: Filamerican Pub., Jan. 1941-Dec. 1950. Formerly Wagayway, Wagayway Filamerican, etc.

Fil-American; The Advocate. V. 1-2, no. 15. San Francisco: Otto E.
     Schalk, July 1952-Mar. 1954.

Fil-American Viewpoint. V.1, nos. 1-2? San Francisco: Jose M. Figueras,
     Dec. 1954-Jan. 1955?

Filipino. V.1, nos. 1-6 Washington: Pub.?, 1906.

Filipino American. V.1-? New York: Pub.?, Mar. 1960-?

Filipino-American Herald. V.1-. Seattle: Emiliano A. Francisco, 1969-.

Filipino Forum. 1-? Seattle: Pub.?, Nov. 1928-?.

Filipino Missionary Messenger. V.1-? Escondido, Calif.: Missionary
     Messenger. Pr., 1937-1954?

Filipino Nation. V. 1-9, no. 3. Los Angeles: Filipino Nation Pub., etc.,
     1926-33. Formerly Equifrilibricum News Service.

Filipino News. V. 1-30, no. 26. Lihue, Hawaii: Filipino News, Ltd.,
     1931-59. Formerly Kauai Filipino News.

Filipino People. V. 1-4, no. 1. Washington: Manuel L. Quezon, Sept.
     1912-May 1916.

Filipino Pioneer. V. 1-2, no. 43? Stockton, Calif.: Pub.?, Sept. 1936-
     Aug. 1938?

Filipino Student. V. 1-2, no. 4. Berkeley, Chicago: Filipino Students of
     America, Dec. 1912-Jan. 1914.

Filipino Student Bulletin. V.1-? New York: Filipino Students in America,
     etc., 1922-?. Formerly Philippine Herald.

Hawaii Medical Journal. V.1-date. Honolulu: Hawaii Medical Assn.,
     Sept. 1941-date. Not exclusively Filipino, but frequently carries
     articles involving racial aspects.

Hawaiian Reporter. Filipino Edition. V. 1-2, no. 40. Honolulu: Pub.?
     June 18, 1959-Mar. 16, 1961.

Hawaii's Filamerican Tribune. V. 1-16, no. 48. Honolulu: Filamerican
     Tribune, ?-Dec. 12, 1955.

Maui Record. V.1-? Wailuku, Hawaii: Maui Record Pub., 1916-36?.

Moncadian. No. 1-? Los Angeles: Filipino Federation of America,
     Spring 1949-?.

Moncado and His Mission Bulletin. V. 1-3, no. 6. Honolulu: Supreme
  Council of Equi Frili Brium Students, Jan. 1955-June 1957.

New Philippines. V. 1-2, no. 5/6. Honolulu: Pub.?, Feb. 1947-Aug./Sept.
  1949.

New Post. V. 1-2, no. 16. Honolulu: Labez Pub., Feb. 1947-June 15/30,
  1949.

Philippine Advocate. V.1-? Seattle: Philippine Advocate Pub., Dec.
  1934-?

Philippine American Advocate. V. 1-3, no. 5. Washington: Pub.?, Jan.
  1937-Aug. 1939.

Philippine-American Journal. V.1-? Stockton, Calif.: Filipe M. Esteban,
  June 1948?-?.

Philippine-American News Digest. V.1, nos. 1-5. Los Angeles: Philippine American Foundation, Apr.-Dec. 1940.

Philippine Commonwealth Journal. V.1-? Portland, Ore.: Philippine
  Commonwealth Jour. Pub., 1939-?.

Philippine Echo. Minneapolis: Philippine Pub., 1927-1931?

Philippine Enterprise. V. 1-2, no. 24? Sacramento, Calif.: Pub.?, Jan.
  2, 1934-May 7, 1936? Formerly Philippines Enterprise.

Philippine Herald. V. 1-2, no. 3. New York: Filipino Students Federation
  of America, Nov. 1920-Mar. 1922. Superseded by Filipino Student
  Bulletin.

Philippine Journal. V. 1-3 (nos. 1-29). Stockton, Calif.: Filipino Agricultural Laborers' Assn., etc., June 7, 1939-Sept. 27, 1941.

Philippine Monthly. V.1, nos. 1-4/5. Seattle: Pub.?, Oct. 1932-Jan./Feb.
  1933.

Philippine News. 1st yr.-date. San Francisco: Alex A. Escamado, 1960-
  date.

Philippine Quarterly. V.1-? Chicago: Pub.?, 1941?-?.

Philippine Republic Press. V. 1-3, no. 12. San Francisco: Evaristo
  Casiano Pecson. Mar. 1947-Feb. 1950.

Philippine Review. V. 1-4, no. 3. Berkeley: Philippine Review Pub.,
  Apr. 1905-1908. Formerly Filipino Students Magazine.

Philippine Review. V. 1-2, no. 18. Seattle: Pub.?, 1930-Dec. 1931.

Philippines in Hawaii. V. 1-2, no 2? Honolulu: Pub.?, 1948-49?

Philippines Journal. V.1-? Honolulu: Pub.?, Dec. 1947-? Known through
     1962.

Philippines Mail. V.1-date. Salinas, Calif.: Gonzales Mail Pub., 1930-
     date. Formerly The Mail, The Mail Advertiser, etc.

Philippines News-Herald. V. 1-9, no. 4? Los Angeles: Victor N. Ramajo,
     June 1940?-Nov. 1944?. Formerly Filipino Eagle.

Philippines Panorama. V. 1-4. Salinas, Calif.: Gregorio C. Aquino,
     Jan. 1957-June 1964.

Philippines Star-Press. V. 1-23? Los Angeles: B. G. Aquino & Sons,
     Feb. 1923?-Dec. 1950?.

Three Stars. V.1-? Stockton, Calif.: Three Stars Pub., 1928-?, Known
     through July 1932.

VI.   Unpublished Materials

Adams, Richard L. Common Labor Needs of California Crops (with
     Special Reference to Mexican Labor). Berkeley: Univ. of Calif.
     Coll. of Agriculture, 1930.

Arino, Vincent A. "Contributions of Filipino Farm Labor to California's
     Industrialized Agriculture." Development Problems in Selected
     California Areas. Berkeley: Univ. of Calif. Dept. of Political
     Science, 1953.

Ave, Mario P. Characteristics of Filipino Organizations in Los Angeles.
     University of Southern California. M. A. thesis. 1956.

Berbano, Marcos P. The Social Status of the Filipinos in the County of
     Los Angeles. Los Angeles: Univ. of Southern Calif. M. A. thesis.
     1931.

Bogardus, Emory S. The Filipino Immigrant Situation. Paper Read at
     the National Conference of Social Work, San Francisco, July 3,
     1929. Los Angeles: Council of International Relations, 1929.

Brooks, Lee M. and Cheng, C. K. Survey of Conditions and Needs Basic
     to Planning a New Jail for the City and County of Honolulu. Pre-
     pared for the Board of Supervisors, Honolulu: n.p., 1955.

Cariaga, Roman R. Filipinos at Ewa. Honolulu: n.p., 1935.

_____. The Filipinos in Hawaii: A Survey of Their Economic and Social Conditions. Honolulu: Univ. of Hawaii. M. A. thesis (no. 128), 1936.

Carrasco, H. C. The Filipino in California. Address under the auspices of the Filipino community of Salinas Valley, Armory Hall, Salinas, Calif., Aug. 2, 1940. Salinas?, 1940.

Catapusan, Benicio T. The Filipino Occupational and Recreational Activities in Los Angeles. Los Angeles: Univ. of Southern Calif. M. A. thesis, 1934.

_____. The Filipino's Social Adjustment in the United States. Los Angeles: Univ. of Southern Calif. Ph.D. Diss., 1940.

Coloma, Casiano P. A Study of the Filipino Repatriation Movement. University of Southern California. M. S. thesis. 1939.

Corpus, Severino Fermin. An Analysis of the Racial Adjustment Activities and Problems of the Filipino-American Christian Fellowship in Los Angeles. Los Angeles: Univ. of Southern Calif. M. A. thesis, 1938.

Dagot, Edilberto P. The Cultural and Linguistic Features Involved in Cross-Cultural Communication between Filipino Students and Americans and the Use of Short Stories to Teach These Features. New York: New York Univ. Ed.D. Diss., 1967.

Directory of Filipino Students in the United States. New York: Filipino Student Christian Movement in America, 1934-1939.

Dorita, Sister Mary. Filipino Immigration to Hawaii. Honolulu: Univ. of Hawaii. M. A. thesis (no. 320), 1954.

Eubank, Lauriel Elsabeth. The Effects of the First Six Months of World War II on the Attitudes of Koreans and Filipinos toward the Japanese in Hawaii. Honolulu: Univ. of Hawaii. M. A. thesis (no. 196), 1943.

Federal Writers' Project, Oakland, Calif. Unionization of Filipinos in California Agriculture. Oakland: Federal Writers' Project, n.d.

Fenz, Walter David. Comparative Need Patterns of Five Ancestry Groups in Hawaii. Honolulu: Univ. of Hawaii. M. A. thesis (no. 473), 1962.

Filipino Agricultural Laborers' Assn. FALA Year Book: Second Annual Convention, July 7-8, 1940. Stockton, Calif.: Filipino Agricultural Laborers' Assn. 1940.

Filipino Community of San Francisco. Day of Our Freedom: a Souvenir Program. Philippine Independence Day Celebration. San Francisco: Filipino Community of San Francisco, 1946, 52p.

Fisk University. Social Science Institute. Orientals and Their Cultural Adjustment. Nashville: Fisk Univ. Soc. Sci. Inst., 1946.

Hawaii Interracial Committee. Report of Hawaii Interracial Committee on Filipino Importation. Honolulu?: Hawaii Interracial Com., 1945.

Honolulu. Filipino Chamber of Commerce. About Your Chamber. Honolulu: Filipino Ch. of Commerce, 1954.

Junasa, Bienvenido D. Study of Some Social Factors Related to the Plans and Aspirations of the Filipino Youth in Waipahu. Honolulu: Univ. of Hawaii M. A. thesis (no. 442), 1961.

Mariano, Honorante. The Filipino Immigrants in the United States. University of Oregon. M. A. thesis. 1933.

Maslog, Crispin Chio. Filipino and Indian Students' Images: Of Themselves, of Each Other, and of the United States. Minneapolis: Univ. of Minn. Ph.D. Diss., 1967.

Miller, Slator M. Report to Mr. H. A. Walker, President, Hawaiian Sugar Planters' Association on 1945-1946 Filipino Emigration Project. Honolulu: n.p., 1946?.

Northern California Committee for the Protection of Filipino Rights. An Appeal to Reason. San Francisco: The Committee, 1940?.

Philippine Society of California. Annual Year Book. (Title varies). San Francisco: Philippine Society of Calif., 1925-32.

Pimentel, Leonila J. The Perception of Illness Among the Immigrant Filipinos in Sacramento Valley. Sacramento State College, M. A. thesis. 1968.

Quino, Valentin R. The Filipino Community in Los Angeles. Los Angeles: Univ. of Southern Calif. M. A. thesis. 1952.

Wallovits, Sonia E. The Filipinos in California. Los Angeles: University of Southern California. M. A. thesis. 1966.

NAME INDEX